THE FATHERS OF THE GREEK CHURCH

By the same Author

THE FATHERS OF THE LATIN CHURCH
English translation in preparation

THE FATHERS OF
THE GREEK CHURCH

BY

HANS VON CAMPENHAUSEN

PROFESSOR OF ECCLESIASTICAL HISTORY
IN THE UNIVERSITY OF HEIDELBERG

ADAM & CHARLES BLACK
LONDON

THIS EDITION FIRST PUBLISHED 1963

A. AND C. BLACK LIMITED
4, 5 AND 6 SOHO SQUARE LONDON W.I

PRINTED IN GREAT BRITAIN
BY R. & R. CLARK, LIMITED, EDINBURGH

Dedicated to

HERMANN DÖRRIES

as one of the fruits of
twenty-five years' friendship

IN PLACE OF A PREFACE

'FRANKLY I do not consider it very difficult, especially in our days, to write a learned book, or what is accounted such, namely a book with learned quotations, notes, explanations and appendages of that sort. It is much harder, in my opinion, to write a book which dispenses with all the apparatus of learning but *presupposes* solid and well-grounded study. I consider this not only much harder, but rarer; for it involves a certain power of renunciation, a willingness to bring oneself to forgo the applause of the many, who judge learning by the outward apparatus. But the rarer it is, in my opinion, the more fruitful and rewarding; indeed I consider it the noblest type of authorship. . . . We have enough and to spare of light-weight, entertaining goods on the one hand and ponderous works serviceable to comparatively few readers on the other; and the cream of the educated Christian public goes empty away.

I have now indicated the ideal that I kept before me in writing this book. No one can be more conscious than I am how far I have fallen short of it. But I have made the effort; and I hope that this will be recognized by the discerning and fair-minded critic.'

FRIEDRICH BÖHRINGER

Die Kirche Christi und ihre Zeugen,
oder die Kirchengeschichte in Biographien,
I, 2 (1842), p. viii f.

CONTENTS

PAGE

Introduction. PATRISTICS AND THE FATHERS OF THE
             CHURCH   1

CHAPTER

   I. JUSTIN   5

   II. IRENAEUS   16

   III. CLEMENT OF ALEXANDRIA   25

   IV. ORIGEN   37

   V. EUSEBIUS OF CAESAREA   57

   VI. ATHANASIUS   69

   VII. BASIL THE GREAT   84

   VIII. GREGORY OF NAZIANZUS   101

   IX. GREGORY OF NYSSA   115

   X. SYNESIUS OF CYRENE   126

   XI. JOHN CHRYSOSTOM   140

   XII. CYRIL OF ALEXANDRIA   158

Conclusion. THE END OF THE AGE OF THE GREEK
             FATHERS   171

Chronological Table   177

Bibliography   179

Index of Proper Names   189

INTRODUCTION

PATRISTICS AND THE FATHERS OF THE CHURCH

THE 'Fathers of the Church' is the term used to describe the orthodox writers of the early Church. Anyone undertaking to write about them does not find himself on new ground but on a very old, oft-ploughed field, and one which has been the subject of fierce controversy. A few indications as to the concept and origins of what is known as 'patristics' or 'patrology' may therefore be appropriate.

The normal task of patrology is the investigation, evaluation, and expounding of the literary and theological achievements of the Church Fathers. It is a kind of literary history of the Church, proceeding alongside and supplementing the history of doctrine and dogma, and forming at the same time an appendix to the literary history of classical antiquity. Patristics did not originate, however, in philology or in the general history of the Church. If it did it would be impossible to fathom the curious limitation of the field imposed by the denominational and theological standpoint of the authors. In fact the term 'Fathers of the Church' itself stems from the sphere of dogma and originated in the needs of Catholic apologetics. Patristics originated in the urge to assemble witnesses to the 'authentic' orthodox tradition, that it might add its weight of authority to valid or disputed doctrines. To this end efforts were made as early as the fourth century to establish the views of authoritative theologians who were expressly described as 'Fathers of the Church'. Their authority was accepted as valid in the present and was added to the earlier and more evident authority of the Bible.

I

This dogmatic interest in ecclesiastical 'tradition' still plays a considerable part in the Catholic Church today. That is the reason why the title 'Father of the Church' is withheld from some teachers, such as Origen, who were fully recognized in their own time. The authority of others, such as Clement of Alexandria, is regarded as uncertain and others, like the Alexandrian patriarch Cyril, are singled out for a position of special distinction as *doctores ecclesiae*. These later classifications constitute a parallel to the corresponding consideration of the canon of Scripture and early Christian literature. In the latter case a series of documents was judged to be 'apostolic' and combined in the New Testament into a dogmatic, authoritative 'canonic' collection, while other writings, possibly just as ancient and originally just as highly regarded, were considered 'apocryphal' or even rejected outright. No attention will be paid to such distinctions in the present work, the intentions of which are wholly historical. Even though they may be ecclesiastically significant and, in the case of the New Testament, entirely justified, it is nevertheless clear that they are irrelevant to the purposes of a purely historical exposition of the Fathers.

On the other hand, an approach limited to the aspects of literary history is certainly not the only acceptable method and is quite inadequate by itself. It has to be remembered that the men with whom we are concerned did not wish in any sense to be thought of merely as writers. They considered themselves the exponents of divine truth, which it was their duty to preserve in the local churches and preach to the world at large. They expressly rejected literary and academic ambitions—such at least were not their main interests in life. They thought of themselves as the authorized teachers of the Church, as Christian philosophers, as trained, enlightened interpreters of the Bible, which contains God's saving revelation. It is in this light that we have to understand and study them. Otherwise, the main purpose of their work and activity will be distorted. This also applies to the historical judgment of their achievement. There can be no doubt that the combination of the Christian and classical inheritance which is the foundation of Western civilization was first created and established by the Fathers of the Church. They meditated on the problem contained in this double legacy and attempted to find a fundamental theological solution. They were not, however, concerned with the much-discussed problem of the adaptation and preservation of the classical tradition: they were concerned with the absolute truth which they found in the Bible and in the tradition of the Church.

The studies which follow are intended to depict the Church Fathers in the light in which they regarded themselves. They are not intended to be read as a summary of the literary history of the early Church or as a short history of Christian dogma. We shall be concerned rather with the personalities, with their intellectual aims, within the context of their own world and age, and with the ecclesiastical function which they fulfilled with their teaching and instruction. The present book is confined to the Church Fathers who wrote in Greek. The Christian literature available to us begins in the Greek world, and Greek theology occupies the leading place in the first four centuries of the Church's history. It develops quite independently, and the self-contained picture which emerges should not be confused by introducing other phenomena, whether Western or Eastern, merely because they were contemporaneous.

It is no accident that the first personality of stature who must be set at the beginning of the series appeared at a time when the idea of the New Testament canon was gradually attaining decisive importance. The Fathers no longer considered themselves direct witnesses of the Christian revelation as did the generation of apostolic and subapostolic times. In all their work they presupposed the witness of that earlier age. They did not write gospels, apocalypses, and apostolic letters but interpretations and treatises, polemical and apologetic tracts of a devotional, systematic, and, occasionally, historical nature, keeping to their own background of knowledge and method. They wanted to serve the Church with their special gifts and abilities, but as entirely free men.

It is more difficult to determine the end of the patristic age than to decide on its beginning. I have decided to place its ending at the point where the work of the Fathers themselves had already established a tradition with a validity of its own, which was restricting the freedom of Biblical and systematic research. This constraining influence led to a change in the method and status of theology. From the fifth century, theology became 'scholastic' in the sense that the authority of the old Church Fathers overshadowed more and more the influence and responsibility of the contemporary teacher.

It goes without saying that the twelve men whom we are to discuss constitute only a small selection of the innumerable host of Greek Fathers; their number could easily be multiplied. But I hope that none of the most significant personalities is missing and that the most essential points in the development of ideas will be represented.

JUSTIN

THE early Church did not engage in theology. It lived on its traditions and the revelations of its leaders and prophets. Their prophecies, instructions, and epistles were imparted to some extent anonymously, with the authority of the Holy Spirit, but later on pseudonymously as well, in the name of the original apostolic witnesses. Theological teachers relying on their own intellectual work, who presuppose a background of scholarly training and strive to defend, establish, and develop Christian truth, appeared only in the course of the second century. This development is inseparable from the influence of the Greek mind, the Greek conception of reason, and the whole tradition of Hellenistic culture. The Greek influence was not merely external, although certain contacts were unavoidable since the Church had become detached from its native soil, spread to the Roman Empire, and become part of its world-wide civilization. As the parallels offered by Judaism and Islam indicate, the acceptance of the Greek legacy was spiritually inescapable and a vital factor in the creation of what we now call theology. The first theologian in this sense was Justin—'the philosopher', as he was called in his own time, or 'Justin the Martyr', because he set the seal on his life as a Christian philosopher with a martyr's death.

It may well be asked whether Justin was really the first to strive to interpret Christianity from the Greek point of view. The history of ideas is in constant flux, and every turning-point, every end and beginning posited by the historians, is a purely symbolic simplification. In fact attempts had occasionally been made before Justin to present the Christian gospel in the forms of a rationalistic 'philosophical' culture, in order to make it available to a wider public. But apart from the earliest attempts recorded in the Acts of the Apostles as recorded by St. Luke, these earlier efforts were so bungling, derivative, and primitive that they can safely be disregarded. Such efforts did not acquire any theological weight and standing until the appearance of Justin, and to that extent he was a pioneer and an innovator though he never made any such claims for himself. It is wrong to place him alongside the other apologists of the latter half of the second century as if he were merely part of a larger group and typical of a general intellectual current. The later champions of Christianity such as Tatian and Athenagoras nearly all learned from him, and he stands head and shoulders above the earlier ones like Aristides and the little-known Quadratus. This was not merely the result of his richer and deeper education; above all, it stemmed from a new and different attitude to education and culture. Justin did not wish only to appear to the heathen in the guise of a philosopher; he wanted really to *be* a philosopher, and what he had to tell them interested him not simply as a Christian apologist but because he has convinced himself first. His Christian philosophy went beyond copying of Jewish and sceptical attacks on idolatry for apologetic purposes; it resulted from his own intellectual development and independent commitment. This is what makes his work so interesting, however many of the details are derivative and in spite of the modesty and incompleteness of his theology as a whole.

According to his own statement, 'Justin the son of Priscus and grandson of Bakcheius' was born in Flavia Neapolis (near Sichem, in Palestine) (*Apol.* I, 1). He once described the Samaritans as his fellow-countrymen, but that does not mean that we must think of him as an 'Oriental'. The old city had been razed to the ground by Vespasian in the Jewish war and had then been rebuilt as a Greco-Roman colony. In any case, Justin was originally a pagan. He seems to have been a typical representative of the urban upper-middle class of the time—

loyal, detached from ancient traditions, and cosmopolitan in outlook, intellectually active and interested, honest of mind and economically independent. Justin did not have to earn his own living; he devoted himself to his intellectual interests and became a 'philosopher'. As such he met the Christians and became one of them. 'This is the only really reliable and useful philosophy that I have found.' His conversion probably took place in Ephesus, where he placed his *Dialogue with the Jew Trypho*. Later on we find him in Rome. It was there that in his fifties he published, among other things, an *Apology* addressed to the heathen, and it was there that he was executed as a martyr about ten years later.

At the beginning of the *Dialogue* Justin gave an elaborate account of the course of his development. He found the superiority of Christianity to reside pre-eminently in the clear knowledge of the true, divine Being, which is possible only if virtue and justice are practised simultaneously. In the *Apology* Justin laid particular emphasis on the Christian love for one's enemies, on Christian patience, chastity and truthfulness, and, above all, fortitude in death. These qualities should, he believed, suffice to dispel the usual calumnies about the Christian way of life, in which he himself had once believed.

Justin's Christianity is marked by an urge to give practical expression to his faith and by the absolute certainty of his ultimate convictions. Christians possess the truth on which to base their lives; this is proved by the high moral standard of their conduct. The sources from which they derive their knowledge of God are, furthermore, undoubtedly reliable. To that extent their teaching fulfils the real mission of philosophy, which, according to Justin, is above all to explore the Divine.

Even more revealing is the criticism which he directs against the pagan schools of philosophy. In his search for the truth Justin desires to explore in all directions, to become acquainted with the whole 'many-headed' monster (*Dial.* 2, 2) of philosophy. He finds the teaching of the Stoics a barren field because they do not go into the real problem of God. The peripatetic philosopher disappointed him even more because after a few days he brought up the question of payment, which is so unworthy of a philosopher. The Pythagorean deterred the seeker after knowledge no less, for he presupposed a mass of musical, astronomical, and geometrical information which Justin neither possessed nor had the time to acquire. In his opinion philosophy should not be a specialized branch of learning, and so in the end he kept to Plato and called himself a Platonist. Nevertheless, he simplified the Platonic philosophy to suit the requirements of the new theology: the main—dualistically tinged—ideas of Platonism which were important for Justin were the pure truth of Being, which is accessible to the pure thinking of Reason; God who is One, beyond the created world, and one with the Good and Beautiful. The average pagan philosopher of the time probably possessed no deeper understanding of what Plato really taught. It is clear that Justin not only read Plato but had, in his own way, a lively understanding of him. In his writings he referred to and imitated him repeatedly. For Justin, as for so many who came after him, Plato became the intellectual bridge leading to the better, 'more ancient philosophers' (*Dial.* 7, 1) whom Plato himself was supposed to have known and used, i.e., the prophets of the Old Testament, and hence Christ himself. Justin henceforth took his intellectual position with them, and Plato became a forerunner and an ally rather than a leader.

Justin's intention, therefore, was not to carry out a kind of philosophical penetration of the Christian message and blend Plato with Christianity. For Justin Christianity was philosophical truth itself; Plato was, in his estimation, already very largely in agreement with the truth of Christianity. God had acted at all times and among all peoples. He had at all times revealed to them, through Christ and outside the confines of the Jewish people, fragments and crumbs of his truth. But in Jesus Christ his eternal reason had appeared in definitive form. Therefore it was possible to say that 'all men who have lived in accordance with reason' had been Christians, including, for example,

Socrates and Heraclitus among the Greeks, and Abraham, Elijah, and many others among the 'barbarians' (*Apol.* I, 46). With one bold stroke the whole history of the human spirit is summed up in Christ and brought to its consummation. Jesus Christ was the Son of God. For this basic Christian dogma Justin gave to the pagans something like a rational philosophical justification, which was intended to dispel the suspicions of polytheism. Christ was the Logos, i.e. divine reason itself, which God the Father suffered to go forth from himself without diminution of his own being. Through him, too, the creation of the world was accomplished. And as the 'Word' of God, the Logos was able in the end even to assume human flesh in order to teach men the perfect truth and wisdom. The surest proof of the truth of these statements lies in the miraculous fulfilment of all the prophecies which occurred when Jesus Christ appeared. In conjunction with the miracles which he wrought and still works today and with the sublimity of the Christian gospel itself, no further doubt about his divine origin is possible. Christ is the new lawgiver who overcomes all demonic resistance and brings unlimited salvation to the world before its approaching end. His suffering and death must not be allowed to confuse our minds, any more than the present persecution which Christians are undergoing, and which is the fate of true philosophers in every age.

It is surprising how Justin takes it for granted that the faith he is defending is a reasonable and all-enlightening knowledge, and how little he is offended by the doctrines that fly in the face of classical philosophy and which had provoked scorn and criticism at all times. The crucifixion of the Son of God, the miraculous effects of his Last Supper, the Resurrection of the flesh, and even the ancient hope of the millennium with the New Jerusalem as its centre—which was already being called in question in the Church itself—all these are accepted by Justin as irrefutable certainties based on the testimony of the Bible, and they clearly offer him no serious problems. It is obvious how firmly and naturally he is rooted in the Faith and the ideas

2

of the Church despite all his philosophical training. It is clear that he regards the validity of the Bible as absolute. Probably this would be still more evident if all his strictly ecclesiastical works, i.e. those expressly written for Christian readers, had not been lost. They were not adequate for a later age and were bound to appear perhaps even dangerous.

Nevertheless Justin knows himself to be a philosopher, and, expressly as a Christian, he now began to teach and be active. He moved into premises of his own in Rome 'above the Bath of Timothy', and he gathered disciples, including some who later became well known as Christian teachers and writers. As an authentic teacher of wisdom, he naturally refused payment for his lessons. He imparted without question the 'precepts of wisdom' to anyone who wished to come to him (*Act. Just.* 3) and continued to wear the philosopher's cloak with pride. Of course from the effects of his teaching he might also be described as a missionary of the Church. But he appeared in public in his own name and no longer worked, like the early Christian teachers, within the religious community, but within the new sociological framework of a private philosophical 'school'. He and his pupils were drawn into the usual competitive struggle of the philosophical schools and cliques, the only difference being that these bickerings now acquired an added intensity and danger because of the religious conflict that raged behind them. Justin himself reports (*Apol.* II, 8 [3]) how he personally challenged the Cynic philosopher Crescens, who had attacked the Christians, and records that he proved the Cynic's complete ignorance, though naturally without avail. The malignant braggart continued to calumniate the Christians and to talk about things he did not understand or did not want to understand; according to Justin he therefore did not deserve the name of philosopher at all. In his *Dialogue* he presents his own conception of a serious philosophical discussion on questions of faith. The Christian and the Jew who here stand opposed both make an effort to conduct the debate in dignified tones and achieve an objectivity and impartiality conducive to rational argument. Each allows the other to have his say, and they both forgo cheap polemical victories. Their sole concern is to arrive at the truth, and this truth must be brought to light in a dispassionate, so to speak scientific, discussion. This is the new 'philosophical' attitude which is also reflected in the pleasant urbanity of the discussion —a quality also derived from Plato. This kind of discussion was beyond the scope of the earlier spokesmen of the Church.

But as we study the contents of the discussion, the connection with the earlier Christian tradition is everywhere apparent, and the philosophical elaboration of the introduction seems an almost accidental and unnecessary disguise. Justin himself in one place says that he is bound to forgo the elaborate rules of methodical and rhetorical exposition. In place of a systematic treatment of the Christian ethic he simply presents, in the arrangement of a catechism, the commandments of the Lord; instead of an exposition of what the Church is, he describes what goes on within it, and what its services are like. Even in purely theological contexts he sometimes contents himself with the traditional formulations—for instance, the Trinitarian Credo. Justin regards his main task as the interpretation of the Scriptures, above all, of the Old Testament. Like the first Christian teachers, he proclaims that he has received the 'gift of grace' for this task from God himself. But he lays particular stress on the importance of his clear and rational method. The merely mechanical repetition of sayings learned by heart is liable to provoke contradiction and contempt. And in yet another respect Justin progresses beyond his predecessors: he wishes to develop scriptural proof to the utmost limit. The *Dialogue* thus becomes a comprehensive compendium of all the Old Testament proof-texts confirming faith in Christ. In this respect it has rarely been surpassed. Needless to say, in this work Justin relies in the first place on the allegorical and typological methods already used in Judaism, combined with a truly rabbinical thoroughness in the assembling of apparently related clues and hidden affinities. The 'tree of life' in Paradise, the rods of green poplar with which Jacob colours the lambs, the

anointed stone 'pillar' of Bethel and all the 'anointed' in
general, the staffs of Aaron and Moses and all the other staffs
and trees of the Old Testament, including the 'tree planted by
the rivers of water' and the 'rod and staff' of which the Psalmist
sings—for Justin these are all clear hints and prefigurations,
'types' of the Cross of Christ and prophecies of Christ himself.
However tiring and complicated such expositions may appear
to us today, written in a laborious and by no means agreeable
style, it cannot be said that Justin lost sight of the broader considerations: he rose above his material. And his concluding exposition of Christendom as the new people of God, of its
holiness and spirituality and the marvellous universality of its
fellowship which embraces the whole world, is particularly
impressive. This interpretation of the Church is another token
of the enlightened and cosmopolitan approach on the basis of
which Justin the philosopher welcomes Christianity as the new
world religion and the unique truth, which must be proclaimed
to his own age.

So much is everywhere apparent: Justin addresses himself to
all men, no matter whether he is speaking in particular to Jews,
heretics, or pagans, and the reason for this is not merely a delight in discussion nor an interest in general intellectual advance-
ment and edification, but it is done to force men to a clear-cut
decision. Truth no longer stands in cool neutrality above the
contending parties: it has become concrete in Christ and it lives
within a particular fellowship, in a particular doctrine, in a particular Word. The fact that in this form it has become accessible
not only to the educated, to philosophers as hitherto understood, but to every man, seems to be a new proof of its perfection. That is why it is supremely important to stand up for
it publicly against all prejudices and calumnies, fearlessly, as
befits a philosopher, and if need be at the risk of life itself. To
be a philosopher means to have a mission and to devote one's
life to it.

Justin's *Apology,* which was written in Rome before the
Dialogue, is the most impressive evidence of this intention. It

takes the form of a formal complaint addressed to the Emperor, Antoninus Pius, and his fellow regents, the Senate, and the whole Roman people. It is an injustice, he declares, that Christians are regarded as a criminal sect and constantly persecuted. Their alleged misdeeds should first be proved; they themselves would then be the last to defend the guilty. In fact they are the most just, most loyal and pious subjects that the Empire has; they are the real and natural allies of the government in its struggle for the peace of the world. An enlightened government would not want to reproach them for refusing to share the corrupt prejudices of superstition. Behind the persecutions for which the heathen mob is responsible there lurk in reality only hostile demons which are afraid of losing their hold over man. Justin was here adopting a popular notion which was already playing a part in philosophical circles, and he merely gives it a new polemical twist. 'Reason directs those who are truly pious and philosophical to honour and love what is true, declining to follow traditional opinions, if these be worthless' (*Apol.* I, 2, 1). Justin thus seeks to appeal to the emperors as philosophers and to remind them of their oft-repeated claims to represent enlightened and up-to-date methods of government. But this *captatio* has nothing in common with mere flattery. 'Do you then, since you are called pious and philosophers, guardians of justice and lovers of learning, give good heed . . . if ye are indeed such, it will be manifested. For we have come not to flatter you by this writing nor to please you by our address, but to beg that you pass judgment after an accurate and searching investigation, not flattered by prejudice or by a desire to please superstitious men, nor induced by irrational impulse or evil rumours which have long been prevalent, to give a decision which will prove to be against yourselves. As for us, you can kill but not hurt us' (*Apol.* I, 2, 2).

The importance of Justin's *Apology* lies in the novel combination of the moral and theological with the legalistic and political elements. It is true that Justin did not fathom or refused to see the ultimate presupposition of the persecutions of the

Christians: the fundamental connection between State and religion which the Roman Empire was bound to take for granted and demand, like every other political organization of antiquity. The rhetoric of his quasi-legal arguments therefore sometimes appears rather artificial and far-fetched. But on the whole his arguments and also his practical references to Christians as taxpayers, to the futility of persecution and the moral painfulness of such proceedings are quite shrewd. It is rather touching to note how eagerly he assumes that everyone is interested in his concerns and presumes, for example, that the emperors have already heard of him and his disputes with Crescens. But instead of smiling at such naïvetés and counting up the blunders which occasionally slip into his long polemical discussions of pagan philosophy and mythology, one ought rather to admire his honesty, the candour and unparalleled audacity with which a man here champions the cause of a community the hopelessness of whose situation must have been perfectly obvious to him. It is not surprising that he finally had to pay with his life.

The account of Justin's end has come down to us. Under the city prefect Rusticus (A.D. 163–67) he was arrested along with six other Christians. He was described as 'reasonable and well informed', and at the trial he was their spokesman. Like his companions, he categorically refused to obey the judge's orders and deny his Saviour, Jesus Christ; after careful examination he had recognized the truth of Christ's teaching and intended to stand by it 'even if it does not suit the people who are slaves of delusion' (Act. Just. 2, 3). He professed his firm belief in the Resurrection and the Last Judgment, and, with the others, he received his sentence unafraid: 'Because they will not sacrifice to the gods and refuse to obey the Emperor's commands, they are to be scourged in accordance with the law and led away to be beheaded (Act. Just. 5, 8).

Justin stands before us as a simple, straightforward, not over-complicated character. He openly states what he believes and what he intends and does not doubt that it is the truth, that the teachings of Christ which he brings mean salvation for the whole world. Neither his relationship to philosophy nor his position in the Church represented a problem for him. It was only later that men slowly came to realize the difficulties which his position entailed. But the life of this 'philosopher and martyr' (Tertullian, *Adv. Val.* 5) was an exemplar. Nearly all the Greek Fathers of the Church were, consciously or unconsciously, his imitators.

CHAPTER II

IRENAEUS

IRENAEUS was a generation younger than Justin and theologically influenced by him. In spite of this, he represents in some ways an earlier type of Christian teaching and ecclesiastical teacher. Irenaeus did not come to the Church from outside with particular problems and expectations: he grew up in the early Church, he knew its traditions and lived for its service. He had no wish to be a philosopher but rather a disciple of the earlier Fathers, an inspired guardian of the authentic apostolic tradition. It is true that the only writings of his that have come down to us were intended for readers within the Church. The situation here is the reverse from that of Justin, who is known to us only as an apologist. Probably Irenaeus too would have given closer study to the problems and tastes of the pagans when he set out deliberately to speak to them. But it is evident that this task was secondary to his activity and writing for the Church. The only apologetic treatise which Irenaeus addressed to the Greeks was, according to Eusebius, 'striking' but also 'very short' (*Hist. Eccl.* V, 26). Apologetics was not the main centre of his interest. That is also obvious from his style of presentation, from the whole tenor of his thought in the writings that have survived. Irenaeus has the manner of an experienced preacher, not that of a philosopher or a missionary wooing his hearers. His style is leisurely, fatherly, edifying, sometimes coarse and jarring. As a writer he is a failure when he attempts to be scholarly or witty, but he succeeds by the warmth, urgency, and earnestness of his basic religious beliefs, which he develops with a convinced and convincing enthusiasm. Irenaeus thus became the prototype of the conscientious pastor and the tireless champion of the Church's teaching. The centuries that followed looked back on him with grateful admiration as the great witness to apostolic truth in a difficult and dangerous period.

Irenaeus came from the old Greek coastal district of Asia Minor. As a boy in Smyrna he had, as he delighted to point out, listened to the sermons of the great bishop and martyr Polycarp, who was regarded as a disciple of the apostles themselves. Here he came to know the genuine, unadulterated gospel, to which he remained faithful throughout his life. When he grew up he became a presbyter in the Church at Lyons. In the year 177 their aged bishop fell victim to persecution at the hands of the mob, and Irenaeus, still comparatively young, was appointed his successor. As such he was at the same time Bishop of Vienne and other small parishes or groups of parishes throughout southern Gaul which were connected with the main centre. Greek, which was Irenaeus's mother tongue, was still spoken here by a considerable part of the population and was understood without any difficulty in all the towns and cities. In the second century Greek was still a sort of ecclesiastical language for Western Christians in general. No one was offended because a citizen of faraway Asia was made a bishop in Gaul. The cosmopolitan character of the Roman Empire and its Hellenistic civilization also helped to carry the Church forward. But it was not tied to one language and culture. In Africa the first Latin sermons were being delivered at this period, and Irenaeus himself, for the sake of his Celtic listeners, sometimes used their own language. In its missionary zeal the Christian Church was even more ecumenical and less prejudiced than the rest of Greco-Roman society, which ignored the 'barbarian'.

The influence which Irenaeus exerted was not limited to Gaul. Just as he himself adhered to the unity of the one Church and proclaimed and extolled it as a divine miracle, his voice was soon heard and heeded throughout almost the whole of Christendom. While he was still a presbyter he was sent with a warm recommendation to Rome by the captive leaders of the

Church at Lyons to deliver a letter which appealed for an understanding of the 'new prophecy' of Montanism. This was a revival movement originating in Asia Minor which was upsetting the whole Church. But Irenaeus was sympathetic toward it. Its old-world belief in the miraculous power of the 'spirit' and its somewhat reactionary moral severity touched a homely and familiar note in his heart, and he did not want to see these pious stirrings of the Church and its 'prophets' liqui-dated without any understanding by official ecclesiastical action. Later on Irenaeus wrote letters in his own name which went to Rome and Alexandria. It was his concern to make peace and mediate between contending parties. When Victor of Rome allowed himself to be persuaded to break off ecclesiastical rela-tions with the Churches in Asia Minor because of long-standing differences about the Easter festival, Irenaeus wrote him a force-ful letter in which he condemned this dictatorial action 'in a befitting manner' (Eus., *H.E.* V, 24, 11).

Differences on practical matters in the Church can be toler-ated without harm being caused; indeed, to a certain extent they merely underline the continuing unity which is created by the Faith. The all-important thing is this ancient Faith itself, the truth of the gospel transmitted by the apostles; but it is never-theless important to be on guard when new doctrines appear, which attempt to steal or falsify the original treasure. Irenaeus personally called to account men whose theology seemed questionable to him; he urged that they should no longer be tolerated as members of the clergy, and to the deacon who re-presented him in Vienne he conveyed dogmatic instructions as to how heretics were to be instructed. Fighting against false doctrines was part of true preaching and an urgent problem to which Irenaeus strove to devote himself throughout his life. His writings were also dedicated primarily to that end.

His chief work, the five volumes of the *Refutation and Over-throw of Gnosis, Falsely So-Called*, was devoted exclusively to the struggle against heresy, and it still remains today the most important source of information about the theological and

sectarian history of the second century. Irenaeus must not therefore be regarded as a narrow-minded and pugnacious fighting-
cock to whom dogmatic quarrels were a necessity for their own
sake. Owing to its rapid expansion in a foreign and pagan
world, the Church at this period had in fact reached a serious
crisis which threatened to change the religious substance of the
Faith and destroy its historical foundations. Only a vigorous
counter-attack could succeed in warding off this danger.
Irenaeus stands, with Justin and various other theologians of his
generation, on one and the same front in this respect. The
enemies they had to fight were to some extent still inside the
Church, but most of them were already outside, split up into
innumerable groups and schools and occasionally united in
clear-cut, self-contained societies of which the followers of
Marcion represented the strongest and most important. The
only thing they seemed to have in common was that they were
altering and attacking what Irenaeus considered the original
apostolic teaching. But in fact, despite all the individual differences, they formed a coherent religious movement at one in its
ultimate impulses and intentions, which pervaded the whole
world of late antiquity. We now describe it as 'Gnosticism'
because its representatives often claimed for themselves a higher,
but in Irenaeus's view 'falsely so-called', religious gnosis, or
knowledge of spiritual mysteries.

The Gnostics turned Christianity into a dualistic escapist religion of redemption and abandoned not only the Old Testament but also the early Christian understanding of the Faith
and the plan of salvation as a lower stage on the road to
perfection. Christ was no longer regarded as a real historical
man of flesh and blood, who brings to fulfilment the promises
of Israel, but as a semi-mythical heavenly Being of cosmic
dimensions. His decisive achievement was the transmission of
the revealing knowledge by which the human soul is torn from
the world of the senses and recalled to its true, eternal home,
to which it must turn again by means of the new knowledge
of the spirit, directly, or with the help of particular sacramental

and ascetic practices. It will thus return to the spiritually divine Being to which Christ bore witness. It will then have no more to do with this world; the Creator God, with his angels, demons, and laws, is the really hostile power from which escape must be sought.

Irenaeus did not succeed in fathoming and fighting the bewildering mass of Gnostic ideas, myths, and speculations in the simplified form in which we have sketched them here. He took the trouble to explore the teaching and origins of each individual sect, which only increased the impression of confusion and intricate fantasy. Irenaeus tried to set out his *Refutation* as systematically and in as much detail as possible. But he himself lacked the clarity, unprejudiced objectivity, and organizing expository power which were needed for the task. Thus the work became the typical example of an unorganized and tiresome attack on heretics which, lacking intellectual superiority, seizes upon every argument which will disparage, cast suspicion on, and caricature the enemy. Their ludicrous pretensions, the contradictions and absurdities of their arbitrary theories, the constant quarrels between their various groups and parties, and, not least, the immoral lives and unprincipled attitude of their leaders are repeatedly exposed. As soon, however, as Irenaeus turns to a positive exposition of the Church's faith, the level of the writing rises and it is clear that he has a true feeling for the fundamental issues in the conflict. He is concerned to repel the blasphemous Gnostic attitude to Creation and to disprove the claim that there is a Jewish creator-God standing over against Christ. In opposition to this the important thing is to grasp the connection of Creation and Redemption, the inner unity of the threefold working of Father, Son, and Holy Ghost in its true meaning.

In the beginning God created and adorned the world with his two hands, the Son and the Spirit, and made man in his own image for this world. True, man and the whole Creation have fallen, but God has not left them fallen. In three stages he has raised man up again: in the Old Covenant the prophets bore witness to him as the Lord, and he has now bestowed on us power to become the children of God through his Son. And at some time to come he will reveal himself as Father in his kingdom. He remains for ever essentially unfathomable, but in love he has come near to us and given us of his spirit. 'It is God's glory that man should live; but it is man's life that he sees God' (*Haer.* IV, 20, 7). This is the key to the meaning of the history of the world, and Redemption does not cancel out, but leads transcendently beyond, Creation. Irenaeus is not urging a cheap belief in progress. Everything in his thought is concerned with the new relationship of sonship which Christ has established. But it is one and the same God who in his triune power fulfils all things and leads the world and mankind to eternal perfection, according to his mysterious decree.

It is not easy to be certain how far such statements are the product of Irenaeus's own thinking. He himself, as we have already seen, set no store on appearing original; on the contrary, he refers throughout his work to the witness of the 'ancients', which he only seeks to preserve and transmit. The best of what he had to give did not grow in his own field. Since this has become apparent, Irenaeus has lost a good deal of his former reputation as a great theologian. All the same, he made the fruits of his reading very much his own and was quite capable of expressing them in his own way. Irenaeus seems most independent where he is no longer fighting heretics on purely dogmatic grounds but attacking them with historical arguments. He treats them as 'innovators' and does not weary of stressing the absurdity and rootlessness of their Christianity, contrasting it with the original and authentic witness of the apostolic faith. The true Church can tolerate no arbitrary alterations to the possession that it has received from the beginning. Needless to say, Irenaeus does not ask whether his own Church, in spite of its historical securities, indeed perhaps because of its absolute commitment to Scripture and the testimonies of the past, may not also have been undergoing a transformation. He contents himself with a reference to the ancient documents as evidence of the authentic message of the Church. If we study the apocalyptic writings of the Gnostics, with their myths and their various apocryphal traditions, we shall be quite justified in concluding that Irenaeus was perfectly right to reject them.

He was the first consciously literary theologian of the Christian Church. He was the first to set the canon of the four Gospels, with a series of further apostolic writings, though not quite the present selection, alongside the Old Testament. Like it, they are quoted as 'scripture'; the two-volume Christian Bible was coming to birth. But the important thing is the basic attitude which Irenaeus adopts toward the Christian Bible, his declared intention of refusing to go beyond that which was revealed in the beginning, and the conviction that the final and irrevocable *depositum* of apostolic teaching is once and for all sufficient for salvation. The texts are unshakable, and Irenaeus wants to defend even his own writings against all attempts to improve on them. The tradition of the Church is no longer an independent factor alongside the Scriptures: it merely confirms the witness of the Bible. When the Gnostics refer to their allegedly secret special traditions it must be stated that they are upstarts and that only the elders of the Church, its bishops and teachers, have maintained direct continuity with the apostles. They must therefore be in possession of the authentic and original tradition. The example of the Roman list of bishops that had recently been established and which Irenaeus records (*Haer.* III, 3, 3) shows this continuity with apostolic beginnings in exemplary fashion, and the splendid unanimity of all orthodox congregations confirms once again where the truth is really to be found.

With this emphasis on catholicity and the succession of the bishops, which the Roman example illustrates so clearly and instructively ('above all others'), Irenaeus introduced ideas which proved especially valuable to the clerical thought of a later ecclesiasticism. He himself only used them as weapons in the fight against the claims of the Gnostics, and apart from this polemical intention he took no further interest in them. For him the Church as a whole is founded directly on the old apostolic word of truth, and, through the Holy Spirit, who gives her his wonderful gifts, she is everywhere united in the spirit. This is particularly evident from a later pamphlet, which has survived only in an Armenian translation, which assembles the main tenets of Christian teaching in an edifying way 'as evidence of the apostolic message'. There is here no longer any mention at all of 'canonical' or official considerations. The Christian message is presented in the simple form of a Bible story, beginning with the Creation and the Fall and leading, by way of the sacred history of Israel, to Jesus Christ, who has redeemed man by his suffering, death and resurrection, and re-newal of life. This decisive event needs no other support than that of scriptural proof from the Old Testament, which Irenaeus, like Justin, expounds again to its fullest extent. Then the apostles spread the gospel throughout the world and estab-lished the Church; she is a new paradise planted in this world. She is impregnated by the Holy Spirit in all her branches, and he makes plain the path of worship and righteousness. The power of idols and idolatry has now been broken and a new life of perfect holiness has begun. Judaism also now belongs definitely to the past. 'For we possess the Lord of the law, the Son of God, and through faith in him we learn to love God with our whole heart and our neighbour as ourselves. But love for God has no part in sin and love of neighbour works no evil on our fellow men' (Epid. 95). The holy Church is protected in its simplicity from all human temptations. Its members know that an ignorant man of God is always better than an impudent Sophist.

Justin had put forward the 'philosophical' claim that Christi-anity could be shown to be truth in an absolute sense even to the rational critical judgment. Irenaeus reminds us that Christianity can nevertheless never be a mere philosophy, that it rests rather on revelation and sacred traditions, that it acts in the Holy Spirit and is transmitted only by the Catholic Church and its apostolic word. With this testimony he is still a fundamentally significant figure, and he continues to influence the Western world especially, even today. His writings were translated into Latin at an early period, then into Syrian and Armenian. His orthodox testimony to tradition was thoroughly approved also by the Greek Fathers of the Church, but although he was a Greek himself his writings fell remarkably quickly into the background and were almost completely forgotten by his fellow-countrymen. His simple, clumsy, and naïve style seemed too old-fashioned and too primitive. The Greek theologians, in seeking a fuller understanding of Christianity and the Church, at once found themselves confronted by new and difficult questions which it was impossible to answer along the traditional lines of communal devotion. They are more 'philosophical' than Irenaeus, and they search for new ways of understanding the old truth and making it intelligible to their contemporaries, in a spirit of astonishing independence.

CHAPTER III

CLEMENT OF ALEXANDRIA

LIKE Justin, Clement of Alexandria came to Christianity by way of philosophy. But the word has a much deeper and richer content for him than for Justin, who in his zealous endeavour to educate and convert always tried to take the shortest road and whose philosophical equipment contained nothing out of the way. No Father of the Church has been judged in so many different ways as Clement. For all his charm and the flexibility of his nature, he had at bottom a complicated or at any rate a many-sided nature containing many strata; he never kept to the beaten track, deliberately avoided established formulas and slogans, and never came to an end with his questioning, research, and thinking. He was a master of discussion, one might almost say a typical man of letters and a bohemian. But he too, in becoming a Christian, has taken a clear, decisive step which gives an ultimate and immovable goal to all his interests and intellectual efforts. Clement too is a servant, and regards it as the purpose of his life to lead men to Christ—a mission which he maintained in a strangely flexible, undogmatically personal way. Clement was not a public teacher of the Church and, despite his extensive knowledge, not really a scholar. He was a man of conversation, a man of spiritual experience, and a cultured pastor of souls. As such he acquired insights, posed questions, and pondered possibilities and problems which we meet almost nowhere else. Some teachers in the Gnostic conventicles may have resembled him, and later on he was read and esteemed in particular by a number of eminent monks. But they were usually bordering on the heretical themselves or had already crossed its frontiers unintentionally. In

3

Clement's own century he was apparently tolerated without difficulty.

We know little about the outward course of his life. He is said to have been born in Athens, but possibly this information is only symbolically correct. Like Justin, he was a traveller and even after he became a Christian he journeyed through all the Greek-speaking provinces of the Empire, from Asia Minor and Syria to lower Italy and Egypt, striving everywhere to further his education. It is characteristic that later on he thought of these journeys as a search for a real 'teacher'. Only the sixth master that he found really satisfied him: Pantaenus, who, in his judgment, surpassed all others in his interpretation of the Bible but who scorned to leave any of his lectures in writing. Like the 'ancients', the teachers of the early Christian period, Pantaenus taught only by word of mouth; it is impossible therefore for us to judge of his quality. *Circa* A.D. 180 Clement met him in Alexandria and there he settled, working as a teacher, like Justin in Rome. Naturally, he was in touch with the Christian congregation, but there is no reason to suppose that he gave lessons on behalf of the Church, as the appointed leader of its catechetical instruction, as tradition relates. His was an independent 'school' with pupils freely enrolled from every camp. Pagans, Jews, and 'philosophers' of all kinds probably came together with educated Christians and Christians with a thirst for education, some of them originally heretics, and all were taught and helped and no doubt many of them were ultimately won for the Church.

Clement thought of himself as an orthodox, Catholic Christian, and rightly so inasmuch as he adopted the most important outcome of the struggle against the Gnostics, the Bible of the Church. He accepted the Old Testament and its belief in Creation, and he strove to base his teaching on the Scriptures. As a theologian Clement, too, was therefore above all an exegete: he regarded the interpretation of the Bible as his real task and vocation. At the same time, however, he took into account all the other theories and 'philosophies' around him and tried to draw them into fruitful conversation. He fought against the false doctrines of the Gnostics and other heretics, but he also studied them and tried to learn from them. His arguments were aimed at instructing and understanding rather than straight-forward 'anathema'. He also lived in a common intellectual world with the pagan philosophers in so far as they were not Epicureans who denied the existence of divine Providence. Once again, Plato stood in the forefront and was regarded as coming nearest to the truth of Christianity.

The metropolis of Alexandria, with its motley, richly ani-mated life, was an ideal spot for the activities of a man like Clement. I am not thinking merely of the academic and, in the strict sense, philosophical culture of the place. The mixture and interchange of cultures, schools, and traditions had been going on here for a long time and had embraced every sort of religion and outlook. Above all it was a place where the theosophical tendencies of late antiquity were able to spread rapidly, here in the vicinity of the ancient Egyptian world of magic.

All this had in the past facilitated the penetration of Judaism, as it was now doing for Christianity, among intellectual circles. It is impossible to understand Clement unless he is seen against this wider background. He was ardently interested in all the ancient revelations, secret traditions, and mysteries, even when he condemned their content, and he thought of Christianity not only as a 'philosophy' but also as a mysterious reality and power which changes and exalts the whole man.

Unlike some of the Gnostic teachers, however, Clement did not become lost in this magical dream world, for he sought for the shudder of the mysterious not for the mere sake of the shudder and the frenzy. He sought in all places rather for the truth, the serious, whole truth which can establish and bind together human life, the truth which signifies for him the knowledge of God, moral decision, and reason, all in one. It was this that he perceived in Plato and apprehended at its most perfect in the earthly 'appearance' of the divine Logos, Christ. Since the coming of Christ all true spiritual life and experience could be but a development of this one clear and inexhaustible, mysterious and yet revealed and recognized, living truth of God.

Clement's literary legacy underwent the same fate as that of all the Fathers of this early period: most of it disappeared. A good deal has survived, however, and enough to enable us to follow this man's curiously versatile mind in the most varied fields. The *Protrepticus* is a Christian missionary tract composed entirely in the style of the ancient philosophical 'admonitions'. Its intention is the same as that of the usual Christian 'apologies' of the second century, but it reached quite a different level and has nothing of the usual swaggering banality of these tracts. According to Eduard Norden (*Die antike Kunstprosa*, 1898[1], 549), even the preface, with its short, rhythmic, ornamental sentences, is one of the most polished products of sophistical prose. With great vigour of spirit it challenges the reader to listen henceforward to the new song whose singer and subject is the new Orpheus, the Logos proceeding from Zion, rather than to the mythical songs in praise of the ancient gods. There follows the traditional attack on the folly and immorality of the pagan myths, mysteries, sacrifices, and images. The relative truth contained in the message of the philosophers is acknowledged. But full, unclouded knowledge is to be found only in the prophets and above all in the Logos, which leads to all truth.

The continuation of this admonition is to be found in the comprehensive *Paedogogus*, or 'Educator'. The purpose of this treatise is to deal with questions of moral and social interest for Christian beginners in an easy, unpedantic manner. The discussion turns above all on practical questions of life and behaviour of great interest to the student of the history of manners: customs of eating and drinking; the life and organization of the home; festivals and amusements; sleep and recreation; make-up and adornment; intercourse in society and between the sexes: all these topics are discussed. A whole chapter is devoted to footwear, another of considerable length exclusively to perfumes, ointments, and garlands. It is clear that Clement took his material very largely from the literature on etiquette that was available to him; nor are his comments on the virtuous and the natural always original. Nevertheless, it is evident that Clement is pursuing a definite line through all the uninhibited chatter and examination of every possible consideration, that he has a goal in view which lies beyond all these apparently trivial discussions.

Christianity must not be thought of as a merely external commandment or requirement which has to be fulfilled according to the letter of the law. It is rather a matter of the heart, of the whole man, and a Christian ethic is an ethic of intention, in its commitment as in its freedom. Clement therefore has no sympathy with radical ascetic ideals. Paul himself reminded us that the Kingdom of God does not consist in eating and drinking (Rom. xiv. 17) nor, therefore, in the abstention from meat and drink, but in righteousness and peace and joy in the Holy Spirit. One can be rich and poor at one and the same time, have possessions and not have them, use the world and not use the world (I Cor. vii. 31). 'Just as humility consists not in the mortification of the body but in meekness, so too abstinence is a virtue of the soul, which has its being not in the visible but in the hidden places' (Strom. III, 48, 3). All external things as such are neutral, adiaphora in the Stoic sense, and the Christian is entirely 'free' in regard to them. But this freedom is not synonymous with caprice and licentiousness. All excess is unworthy of a man, and therefore of a Christian. Clement can explain the fact that Jesus' feet were anointed with precious ointment (Luke vii. 37 f.) only by pointing out that the woman who anointed them was unconverted. He uses an allegory to interpret the incident: the extravagant ointment typifies the divine teaching which was to be carried out into the world by the feet of Jesus, i.e. by his apostles. In general, moderation, self-control, unobtrusiveness, usefulness, and common sense are to be commended as Christian virtues, the practice of which is always seemly and therefore to that extent in accordance with the requirements of philosophy. However, the ultimate power which governs Christian freedom is not mere reason but the love that loves God and therefore neighbour also and gives him willingly all that he needs. This love, which had already been enjoined on man in the Old Testament, is in accord with justice and common sense, the basic concepts of the social philosophy of the ancients.

It is understandable that Clement has always been a favourite of all humanists. He wishes to keep faith with the classical, Hellenistic ideals, and the fact that he always tries to give sound philosophical and rational as well as Scriptural reasons for what he has to say should not be dismissed as mere conformism. For him there is no irreconcilable antithesis between the two. The classical philosophers and the 'barbaric' prophets of the Old Testament seem to stand almost completely in line with one another as pioneers of the truth which was revealed in Christ. No people was ever utterly forsaken by Providence, and ultimately 'the one true God is the sole author of all beauty, whether it is Hellenic or whether it is ours' (*Strom.* I, 28). The fact that many 'weeds' are to be found in the philosophers, unlike the Bible, and that 'not all nuts are edible' (*Strom.* I, 7, 3) does not affect this fundamental insight. Clement refuses to be in the least intimidated by the anxious spirits who mistrust science and scholarship and are afraid of Greek philosophy 'like children who are frightened by the black man' (*Strom.* VI, 80, 5). If we add that he rejects the demands of asceticism with absolute determination and affirms the noble enjoyment of earthly goods as natural and according to the will of God ('Why should I not enjoy them? For whom have they been created if not for us?' [*Paed.* II, 119, 2]), he seems to be almost the prototype of a liberal theologian, with his worldly piety. But in fact Clement was no more a liberal than he was a pietist. He strove deliberately to reach out beyond both these basic attitudes, extolling Christianity as a religion on its own, which towers above paganism and Judaism alike. Christianity is newness of life from a new Being which is perfect above all former ways of life, beyond all mere rationalism and legalistic morality. It is a new enthusiasm of fellowship with God in faith, hope, and love, and it is therefore the crowning of all human culture and religion: it is perfection of life in God.

To know Clement thoroughly it is necessary to turn to his *Stromateis* ('Patchwork', 'Carpetbags'), which is a wide-ranging work really leading nowhere in particular, the strangeness of which only increases as one gets to know it better. Even the external form of the work, in which no clear plan can be detected, seems rather puzzling. The title sets it among similarly assorted productions of the classical writers known as 'tapestries', 'embroideries', 'meadows', or 'helicons'. They are miscellanies, preliminary studies and drafts, which were developed into a kind of art form in Greece. In the last, the eighth miscellany (Carpetbag), the material is not arranged at all: it consists entirely of preliminary drafts and excerpts which Clement intended to make use of later on. It may be asked, however, how far the *Stromateis* was intended for a wider public at all. Perhaps it represents the teaching material of the Clementine school, and as such it may be able to give us an idea of his methods of instruction, rather in the manner of lecture notes. All the same, the literary intentions of the work seem to go beyond that. The content of these 'Carpetbags' is extremely varied but always related to certain fundamental and central questions. Clement deals, for example, with the significance of classical philosophy, and he discusses faith and knowledge, the love of God and problems of marriage and virginity. Longer sections deal with the purpose and meaning of true martyrdom, the Christian testimony of word and blood. Clement discusses particular doctrines of the heretics; he refers to the tradition of his own teachers and the 'elders' and Fathers of the Church. Finally, he turns with especial love and sympathy to the picture of the perfect 'gnostic', the Christian who is completely at one with God in knowledge and love. The word 'gnostic' is therefore by no means limited in this context to the heretics, as it often is in modern usage. On the contrary, Clement's whole conception of Christianity is consummated in the ideal of the 'knowing' Christian.

It is well-nigh impossible to discern a continuous line of thought running through the 'Carpetbags'. But the greatest difficulty arises from the constant change not only of subject but also of point of view, style, and intellectual level. The point of reference is again and again the Bible, echoes of which even unintentionally pervade the whole of the discourse. But poets and philosophers are also quoted in great abundance, and Clement follows them very closely over long stretches. He deals with objections and differences of opinion; he seems to oscillate backwards and forwards, in a perpetual conversation, to ask questions, listen, discuss, and then continue on his own, after making a few reservations. He is not afraid of forming judgments and taking up his own position; but these are often merely provisional; he seems never quite to exhaust the subject, and he often refers the reader to expositions which are to come later. One has the impression that what he has in mind is an ultimate whole towards which he is steering, but which eludes him again and again, which he finds it impossible to grasp. The ambiguity and confusion of the exposition, which impel the reader to further thought and questioning, are, however, quite intentional. Clement is indeed not a strictly systematic thinker, but it would be doing him an injustice to interpret his commitment to this odd style as a shamefaced confession of his own helplessness or even as a careful evasion of the criticism which might be provoked by this free and literary discussion of sacred matters.

Clement stated at the beginning of the work, and many times quite clearly elsewhere, why he had to make a principle of irregularity and so often changed his standards and points of view. The method follows from the nature of the cause it is intended to serve. Christianity cannot simply be taught, at any rate it cannot be communicated by writing and made available to everyone once and for all. Its reality is mysterious and is fully revealed only to those who are ripe for it and sufficiently blessed by God. Faith must be appropriated by each new person and is not spread but only desecrated by overhasty publication. The 'Carpetbags' therefore constitute a deliberate thicket, a 'spiritual park' where fruitful and unfruitful trees are planted higgledy-piggledy, so that the merely inquisitive and the hypocrite cannot steal the fruit but those who are inwardly prepared will immediately find and enjoy them. Clement is content if he has written for one reader who really understands him, but this reader will understand him not merely by reading him but on the basis of his own living experience and an inner affinity which discovers that to which it is akin.

As we can see, there is more to Clement than the usual mystery-mongering of arcane disciplines and queer disguises. He is concerned, albeit in the fashionable outer garb of such ideas, with 'truth as an encounter' and an experience, with the difficulties and possibilities of an individual and existential communication and appropriation of the truth. This was a problem with which Plato had already wrestled, when he deliberately renounced the direct, dogmatic communication of his teaching by writing. Clement is therefore quite justified in referring to him.

Real life-establishing knowledge has to be acquired personally; it can be taught, shown, and witnessed only personally, by word of mouth, in direct responsible encounter. The ultimate knowledge cannot be acquired from books, and it should not be revealed in books. One does not put a knife into the hand of a child. That is why the teacher's personality is so extraordinarily important and so absolutely indispensable for a living Christianity. Clement urgently exhorts everyone to choose such a spiritual guide and friend as will tell him the truth quite openly, and who is not afraid, if the need arises, to buckle to in earnest, as a means of helping and healing. In the sphere of higher religious knowledge the figure of the teacher attains even more far-reaching importance. He is not merely the vigilant teacher, the Socratic helper and partner on the way to an independent appropriation and appreciation of the truth;

as the man who has been caught and consecrated by God, he is the proper mediator of the truth, the first to make it really alive and visible to the beginner. By gradually introducing him to the new world of Christian prayer, vision, and love he transforms the seeker and the simple believer and so for the first time turns him into an understanding, ardent, and radiant 'knower' of his Lord. Measured against these ultimate realities and experiences, all merely theoretical knowledge can be no more than a preparation, a kind of pre-knowledge and pre-understanding, like such aids to philosophy as geometry and other *propaideumata*. Even a Christian book, indeed the very Bible itself, in which all wisdom is contained, cannot simply as a book replace the teacher. The fire of the spirit can be kindled only by a living fire.

Perfection is attained at the highest level of knowledge. The perfect gnostic no longer needs the human teacher, since he has become directly linked with God through the Logos and thereby become the friend and intimate of God. He has been raised far above the cares and passions of this world; they no longer reach him, although outwardly he continues to live freely and without constraint in the world. He is no longer lured or frightened by visible things. Through the inner attachment of his will to God he has entered the choir of eternally adoring angels. He may travel and associate with other people, rest, read, engage in business—but basically his whole life is an uninterrupted prayer, a continuous intercourse with God, a constant feast. God always hears this striving toward him, though it may not be expressed in words. The true gnostic, however, no longer lives for himself in this state of blessed perfection. In his love for God, the love of God lives in him; he becomes the living, active image of Christ and descends with joy to his fellow-men who are all—like him—called to the Highest and are to enter the kingdom of divine knowledge through him.

In this praise of the perfect gnostic Clement is describing himself, the ideal which he tried to realize with his pupils who saw in him their teacher, pastor, and pattern. Clement hardly

ever mentions the wider fellowship of the Church and its
organization. When he does speak of clerics and their tasks,
as the Old Testament texts necessarily invited him to do, they
automatically become types and allegories of the degrees of
spiritual perfection by which he is exclusively preoccupied.
Fundamentally, the officials of the Church do not interest him.
The gnostic and the gnostic teacher are the really priestly characters, and the spiritual legacy on which they feed cannot be
transmitted through official channels. This relative disregard for
the clerical and ecclesiastical must not be interpreted, however,
in the sense of a rejection or an expression of secret hostility.
On one occasion Clement himself says that the genuine gnostic
should not shun the public worship of the Church, even if he
no longer needs it himself. We even have a lengthy sermon
which Clement himself preached. To be sure, it is not clear
whether this was a sermon actually delivered in church or a
kind of 'Bible lesson' or religious lecture meant only for a
limited circle of his own pupils. Here at any rate we can see
how well Clement understood how to develop a train of
thought with perfect simplicity and clarity when necessary and
bring it to its conclusion without any ostentatious frills and
with real feeling. But the academic level of the sermon and the
problem it deals with seem aimed at particularly high levels of
Christian society. Clement shows in connection with the peri-
cope of the 'rich young man' that it could not have been Jesus'
intention to exclude the rich from the Kingdom of God altogether. Here again, the issue is fundamentally inward and
spiritual—namely, the loosening of the heart from the bonds
of earthly greed. Once this has been achieved, riches, rightly
used, are a good thing and can even become a means of eternal
salvation. No one should despair of achieving this end. The
sermon concludes on a lively and moving note, with the story
of the 'young man who was saved' (which Herder turned into
a German poem). The old story of the apostle John, who wins
back for the Church an unfaithful disciple who has become the
leader of a band of robbers, illustrates the boundlessness of the

divine forgiveness, the rescue of the apparently lost by the force of repentance and the marvellous power of the transforming Christian gospel.

Toward the end of his life we lose track of Clement again. He did not stay to the end in Alexandria, where he had lived for so long. In the year 202 or 203 he left it for good, it appears, to escape from the hardships imposed by measures instituted against the Christians and their missionary propaganda, which were intensified under Septimius Severus. About the year 211 we hear from Cappadocia that in that place Clement had 'strengthened the local church and extended its knowledge' and had travelled from there to Syrian Antioch bearing a message from the Church (Eus. *H.E.* VI, 11, 5 f.). He must have died soon after this, since about the year 215–16 the former Cappadocian Bishop Alexander already included 'holy Clement', his excellent 'master and brother', with Pantaenus, among the 'fathers who have gone before us' (Eus. *H.E.* VI, 14, 8 f.).

The later Church scorned to include Clement among its recognized saints. Too little was known of him, and some of his teaching seemed suspicious. He was judged far too much from the standpoint of a different age. He deserved to be remembered more favourably by posterity. But the lack of enthusiasm is understandable when one remembers that of all the Fathers of the Church, Clement was without any doubt the 'most unecclesiastical' of all, in other words, the one who was most indifferent to the organized Church. And yet, even as early as his time, the question of the Church—its law, its functions, and the orthodoxy of its preaching—was becoming more and more important everywhere. Henceforward, it was no longer possible to treat these matters, as he had done, as of more or less secondary importance, or simply leave them alone. Living Christianity now came to be understood in terms of the Church and not as a matter of purely personal training and knowledge, the teaching of extravagant personal spiritual perfection.

CHAPTER IV

ORIGEN

COMPARED with the achievement of Origen, the work of the earlier Fathers of the Church seems a mere prelude. According to their personal background and character they single out from the profusion of early Christian traditions the things that appeal to them most, and these they commend to the pagan world with missionary zeal, orienting themselves to the requirements and expectations of the educated and extolling Christianity as the fulfilment of all wisdom and religion. They think of themselves as preachers of the truth that has been revealed, and the Bible, freely interpreted, is their one firm support. But they nowhere establish a systematic body of theological thought, and with the exception of Clement their use of philosophy and learning is somewhat amateurish and determined by their own particular apologetic and polemical interests. They did not realize the problematical nature of their position in the Church.

The most important of these men was Hippolytus of Rome, who worked for part of the same period as Origen (until the year 235). Hippolytus was a pupil of Irenaeus and probably, like him, a native of the East. He became a Roman presbyter and bishop at Rome, and as such he felt a proud sense of responsibility for the representation and defence of the old Catholic tradition which derived from the apostles. Hippolytus was also a 'philosopher' and a profound scholar who wrote, besides his sermons, the first continuous commentaries on the Bible and also a chronicle and calendrical tables. His followers put up a statue in his memory which shows him teaching on his bishop's throne, with a catalogue of his works on the sides.

But respectable though Hippolytus's philological studies and dogmatic zeal may have been, all in all he was far too rudimentary and superficial to be able to create the comprehensive intellectual and ecclesiastical self-confidence which the Christians needed in the new century. Origen was the first to bring this about.

Apart from the pagan Plotinus, he was the most comprehensive mind of his time and he appeared at a historical turning point when the Church was abandoning the narrowness of a conventicle-like existence forever and the points were being set for the future. By moulding the outlook, ideals, and Churchmanship of his contemporaries he determined the direction of Greek theology for more than a century, influencing its destiny and contributing to some extent to its ultimate catastrophic downfall.

We are much better informed about the life and work of Origen than about his predecessors. Eusebius devoted practically the whole of the sixth book of his *Church History* to him and was able to draw on Origen's own library in Caesarea, which contained his entire literary estate and also the letters that are now missing. Of his writings, which are said to have numbered thousands, a considerable quantity has survived, although many of them are now extant only in translations and anthologies in which the most audacious and therefore the most offensive of his ideas have been omitted or 'improved'. We must confine ourselves here to the most important of his ideas.

Origen was probably the first Christian writer of whom we know for certain that he came from a Christian home and was given a Christian education. Like Irenaeus, Origen did not come to the Church from outside, he did not seek for bridges and approaches to open it up and make it intelligible to the world: the Christian faith was for him a given fact, the centre of truth from which he looked at everything. His intellectual development proceeded without fanaticism and without compromise, without a break, smoothly, and without pause. One has the impression that this man—whose life, as Eusebius says,

is 'noteworthy from his swaddling clothes onwards' (*H.E.* VI,
2, 2)—never lost a moment's time and never suffered any
spiritual checks. The intellectual tendency also came from his
parents. His father, Leonides, had been a teacher in Alexandria
and would certainly have taught his own son not only the
'encyclical' subjects—mathematics, grammar, rhetoric—but
also the beginnings of Christian knowledge. In the year 202 he
fell victim to a persecution of the Christians. Origen, who was
about seventeen or eighteen at the time, had encouraged his
father in a letter not to weaken or give in for the sake of his
wife and children. According to a legend, he himself escaped
martyrdom only because his mother hid his clothes and so pre-
vented him from going outside. Such were the auspices under
which he entered into adult life. He had nothing of the carefree,
sometimes almost playful enjoyment of culture so typical of
Clement, who was escaping from persecution at this same time.
Behind the gigantic work of scholarship which he was to
achieve there was from the very beginning an austere and
ascetic earnestness and the iron resolution of a man who never
lost sight of the possibility of martyrdom. It may be that in his
youth his enthusiastic radicalism bordered on the heretical.
Basing his action on a word of Jesus (Matt. xix. 12), Origen
took the step, of which he himself later disapproved, of castrat-
ing himself 'for the sake of the Kingdom of God'. From the
beginning, however, he was a member of the orthodox Church.
He joined it in Alexandria and remained loyal to it later on,
even on the long journeys which, like Justin and Clement, he
made to Asia Minor, Greece, and Rome.

To begin with, Origen also became a teacher, concentrating
even more than his father had done on Christian instruction.
There was a lack of Christian teachers and teachers of Christianity, since persecution had affected them more than anyone
else. Origen was not deterred, and Demetrius, the vigorous
Bishop of Alexandria, recognized his quality and secured him,
in spite of his youth, for the regular instruction of catechumens.
Under his direction this semi-official school acquired a rapidly

growing importance and, so to speak, academic status. It was also attended by heretics and pagans, needless to say, free of charge. Origen lived on the proceeds of the sale of his father's library of pagan authors, drawing a modest annuity just sufficient for the life of an ascetic who was constantly working and denied himself all unnecessary pleasures. Origen did not, however, keep to this path for ever. Although he won the admiration of his friends, he was not content with the training he had had and decided to become a student again and study the encyclical sciences, and, above all, philosophy.

This could be done only at the feet of pagan teachers, and Plotinus's master, Ammonius Saccas, appears to have been Origen's teacher too for about five years. In his school Origen met the future Alexandrian Bishop Heraklas, whom he secured as a colleague in his own school. Later on, he left the teaching in the lower part of the school entirely to him and devoted himself to the higher philosophical, theological, and Biblical teaching of his more advanced pupils. After the break with Demetrius, Heraklas succeeded Origen as director of the school.

The importance of these years of philosophical study for Origen can hardly be overestimated. Origen was the first Christian to join the intellectual élite of his age, drawing attention to the teaching of Christianity in a way that forced even his enemies to take notice. No less a man than Porphyry, the biographer of Plotinus, testifies to this with mingled admiration and exasperation. Origen, he thinks (Eus. *H.E.* VI, 19, 7 f.), professed the teaching of the barbarians and lived as a Christian contrary to the laws; but nevertheless in his view of God and the world he was Hellenistically-minded. 'He was quite familiar with the writings of Numenius, Cronius, Apollophanes, Longinus, Moderatus, Nicomachus, and the celebrated Pythagoreans.' Only, 'unfortunately', in the opinion of the pagan Hellenes, he 'introduced Platonic ideas into foreign myths'; in other words, he interpreted them as affirmations of the Jewish-Christian Bible.

Naturally, Origen himself would never have agreed with

this description. He studied the pagan philosophers in order to be able to refute them, and he was firmly convinced that he had himself earlier and more completely drawn from the Christian revelation whatever elements united him with them. He cannot, however, have thought the methodical study of philosophy useless, since he also made it a compulsory subject for his students. It may therefore be asked whether his opponents' pungent judgment of him was not in fact justified. Origen offers the first great example of a theology which, while its intentions are exclusively Christian, nevertheless unconsciously runs the danger of falling into line with the enemies which it takes so seriously—at the time with Neoplatonism which was just arising, as with many later thinkers like Kant, Hegel, or Heidegger. It is impossible to give a straightforward yes or no to the question whether a theology of this kind is Christian or not. Even in Origen the blending of the elements is far too organic and complicated to make a simple answer feasible. In contrast to modern philosophical developments, the Middle Platonic philosophy of that period had not yet been influenced and conditioned by Christianity; but it was sustained to an increasing degree by the same Gnostic atmosphere that permeated and directed the Christian thinking of late antiquity. Theological and anthropological problems such as theodicy, moral development, the doctrine of immortality, the demand for withdrawal from the material world, the problem of the meaning of the material world's decay and its possible return to the original Divine unity, the investigation of the concept of Being itself with these considerations predominating—all these were topics and problems which forced themselves to the front and were interpreted as the basic problems of Platonic philosophy, just as they were, in Origen's view, the basic problems of Christianity itself.

On the whole, historically considered, Origen was in advance of the philosophical developments of his time, in the questions he asks and the answers he gives. His point of departure was different in so far as he was already able to proceed from the

4

reality of an all-sufficient divine revelation based on the testimony of the Bible. Jewish theosophists and 'philosophers' such as Philo of Alexandria, Christian Gnostics and theologians such as Clement, had preceded him, and even the pagan philosophers had long been interested in the sacred wisdom of ancient myths and mysteries and had made a start with an allegorical-philosophical interpretation of the Homeric epics in particular. If one looks, for example, at the doctrine of angels and demons in which Origen was vitally interested and which the Neoplatonists were in the habit of treating as an important part of their theology and interpretation of the world, it is quite impossible to separate its origins and paths of development and influence with any certainty. The new element which Origen gave to the Church was primarily the great systematic summary. He was responsible for the change from an occasional and superficial interest in philosophy to a methodical study of intellectual problems, from the aphorism of educated discussion to the responsible construction of a well-established theological system. There is not a sentence in Origen which was written perfunctorily, not an idea that cannot be taken seriously and followed up further. Just as he led his own students in a careful educational plan through the study of logic and ontological 'physics', of geometry and astronomy to ethics and thence to theology proper and the study of the Bible, the holy essence of the spiritual universe, so in his system of thought every single idea is set and examined within a broad context of knowledge.

None of the later Greek Fathers achieved this integration to the same degree. Origen is the only one to present the whole of Christianity in the form of a workable philosophical system. In the first Alexandrian period of his life, when he was about forty years old, he wrote his most characteristic work: *Peri archon* (Latin: *De principiis*), a Christian work on dogma 'about original things' (or 'about the main doctrines'). Admittedly, the boldness of this essay inevitably brings to light the problematical nature of Origen's whole theology. The Christian gospel can be brought into the framework of an objectified doctrine

of God and the world only with the help of a radical reinter-
pretation of its content. The tradition of the Church, with its
mythology and scheme of redemption, is blended with the
abstract categories and value-concepts of philosophy into a
strange mixture—a kind of cosmically theosophical history of
the spirit and revelation which is developed along speculative
lines on the basis of certain Biblical postulates.

The work has not come down to us entirely in its original
form. At the outset Origen asserts that he does not intend to
deviate by a hair's-breadth from the teaching of the Church;
what in fact he offers, however, is more like a Gnostic myth of
the fall and rise and passing of the world, the only difference
being that the myth is very largely transposed into philosophical concepts and interpreted more or less 'symbolically'—a
kind of demythologizing which brings the whole thing very
close to the later neoplatonic system of Plotinus. To begin with,
the doctrine of God is considered—God, who is the absolute,
immutable spiritual substance, the original unity, who must
also be thought of as the original living Being and eternal
Creator. From him the Logos arises eternally as his image.
Through the Spirit the divine nature is extended to the Trinity,
and finally, through the Logos, God creates the unbounded
world of spirits, who surround him, loving and beloved. As
personal beings they are free; they can therefore also abuse their
freedom and commit the sin of departing from God. By their
doing so, the world comes into being, advancing into ever
wider circles in a process of 'cooling off', of becoming estranged
from God amidst ever-increasing darkness until the stage of
corporeality is reached in which the fallen spirits—human souls
are also pre-existent—are enclosed as a punishment and a puri-
fying prison. But fallen Creation is always sustained and guided
by the providence of God who ceaselessly strives for the
recovery of the apparently lost. The sending of the Logos,
Christ, who is united with a pure human soul, is a decisive
event in this process. At the end of the process, because evil
is not a positive power and can have no lasting reality, even

the blackest devils of hell are completely restored to God. Like all sin, punishment, and pain, evil is only a dark transition leading, by God's guiding care, to the best in the end. Freedom and with it the possibility of recovery can never be lost.

[Origen does not acknowledge the existence of 'absolute evil' or the possibility of eternal separation and damnation.] The heretical nature of this idealistic conception is increased by the fact that for him the final restoration of the Kingdom of God can hardly consistently form a final and absolute end. It follows from the nature of spiritual freedom and from the character of divine education (which leads but never forces) that new darknesses and new eras of redemption may be unleashed in the infinite distances of time. But Origen did not stress this idea. To him time itself is not an ultimate, seen from God's point of view. (The true life lies beyond time, in eternity.) In our earthly state, however, we are not in a position adequately to grasp this eternal being. When Origen does actually overstep the limits of the Christian revelation he is quite well aware that all his speculations are indubitably marked by an element of metaphor, imagery, and poetry. But he does not doubt that in this way he approaches more closely to the truth contained in the Bible than he would if he simply kept to the literal 'disguised' assertions of its anthropomorphism, as the simple unphilosophical mass of the faithful are in the habit of doing.

The anthropology and ethics suited to this metaphysic display the same idealistic and ascetic characteristics. By the knowledge of its origin and vocation which Christ has brought, every single soul is summoned to loose itself from the fetters of this visible world and to begin the return journey and ascent to God in new holiness. Origen does not keep to cool description and contemplation. He thinks of himself as a missionary and pastor of his students and tries to train them to become men of prayer, martyrs and saints. Everyone must, as a spiritual warrior, join the ranks of the Christians, the spirits and angels on God's side, and take up arms against the vices and demons of the world. (There are various forms of service and help; but the decisive force leading to salvation and victory remains gnosis, the full knowledge of divine truth. It is only truly to be found in Christ, the teacher and pattern of all Christians. He meets the soul, as the soul requires; he makes plentifully available in the Church spiritual helpers and means of grace. But the soul must make its own decision, and in the final resort it is by the innate capacity for spiritual freedom that the truth is known and redemption obtained.

This conception of freedom and guidance not only confirms the immortal spiritual dignity of man; it also serves to justify the ways of God and the apparently imperfect divine government of the world. The idea of theodicy occupies a good deal of space in Origen's work and establishes a clear relationship between his theology and the contemporary systems of Middle Platonism. There is no room left for the genuinely Christian conception of judgment, sin and forgiveness, or even redemption in the strict sense of the word. Origen does not realize how the Biblical concepts are transformed under his hands, believing that he is only trying to understand them more deeply. It almost seems as though the Christian character of his outlook is shown only in the greater warmth with which he professes his belief, and the personal devotion and cordiality with which he strives to win new believers. Origen describes the process of redemption less anthropologically than the philosophers, that is to say, not simply as a myth of the Fall and the possible return of the soul to its home, but theologically, as the expression of a divine purpose of love and guidance. In the end, however, these are mere nuances and slight differences in emphasis within the same basic view of life. The only decisively Christian factor is that Origen—contrary to the formal logic of his system—never fails to relate all knowledge and sanctification to the person and pattern of Christ and that the Bible remains the all-important document, guarantee, and support of his faith. In this he follows the line of the earlier Christian 'teachers', and no philosophical scorn for the barbarism of his 'myths' ever disturbs him.

The last section of his main work introduces an explicit justification for this procedure: a detailed theory of the Scriptures and the principles by which they should be 'spiritually' interpreted.

Like all the early Fathers, Origen must be judged primarily as a Bible theologian inasmuch as the great bulk of his literary work, which reflects his method of instruction, consists of Biblical exegesis. It is true that, besides the *Peri archon*, it is possible to name a few further theological monographs of smaller compass: on the Resurrection, on prayer, on martyrdom, and also a work, which has unfortunately disappeared, with a title we have already met—*Carpetbags*—which is said to have contained a sort of Harmony of Biblical and philosophical doctrines. But apart from the fact that these writings also consist very largely of exegesis, they almost vanish beside the mass of extended Biblical commentaries, shorter 'scholia', for the most part explaining individual points, and the homilies, or sermons, which deal sometimes with whole books of the Bible, consecutively. About a third of these works have survived but nothing at all of the 'scholia' commentaries in connection with them. As a Biblical scholar Origen did not confine himself, however, to exegesis. With his usual care he sought to set everything on a broad and firm foundation, and so as a first step he made for his own use a comprehensive edition of the text of the Old Testament the so-called *Hexapla*, or sixfold edition. Alongside the unvocalized Hebrew text it gave first of all a Greek transliteration, to preserve the original sounds, and there followed in further columns the various Greek translations—above all, the venerable Jewish Alexandrian translation of the Septuagint (LXX), the deficiencies and additions of which were specially indicated by the usual signs. As a rule the edition offered four translations, making altogether six narrow columns, which it was possible to compare at a glance. But in certain cases Origen added a fifth, sixth, or seventh translation. Of one such text he remarks incidentally that it was found in a pitcher near Jericho. The modern sensational discoveries in the caves by the Dead Sea therefore had their predecessor in the third century.

The so-called *Tetrapla* (an extract from the *Hexapla*) was produced for a wider circle of readers. This contained only the four Greek translations, without the Hebrew text. The original of the *Hexapla* itself was probably never reproduced. But one hundred and fifty years later Jerome was still able to use it in the Catholic library in Caesarea, and he was especially struck by the corrections which Origen had made in his own hand.

In his exegetical work Origen was therefore able to refer from time to time to this solid manuscript foundation. His exegesis was intended to be a strictly scientific achievement, especially in the great *Commentaries*. In the matter of sheer detail they are not inferior to any modern commentary. The interpretation of the Gospel According to St. John (as far as Chapter xiii, verse 33) covers no less than thirty-two 'volumes'. The explanation of the first six words, 'In the beginning was the Word', required a whole volume. Origen attached not the slightest importance to literary decoration or rhetorical effects. He was not artistic by nature, and he despised 'the teachers who never want to do anything but compile well-sounding statements and resounding sentences' (*Hom. Ezech.* 3, 3). He is concerned exclusively with the matter in hand. He puts the questions and gives his answers quietly and in a clear and orderly manner. He deals in detail with differing views and shuns no delays or detours where they seem necessary for a proper understanding. Now and then he discusses problems of textual criticism and historical background. Generally speaking, however, this occurs but rarely and is quite secondary. The real interest is of a purely theological-systematic nature.

The Bible is the authoritative document behind all Origen's teaching and research: the inexhaustible source of all metaphysics and ethics, all theology, philosophy, and scientific knowledge. Origen is convinced that in its present form the Bible, as the book of the Church, represents a wonderful and many-sided whole which God has created by direct inspiration. He interprets the inspiration behind the Bible not as 'testimony' that is, the deposit of a sacred history or a profession of belief on the part of its human authors, but as the timeless essence of the divine revelation itself, 'a sea of mysteries'. The individual narratives and words are explained to the last detail and made to express new and sometimes extremely surprising mysteries. We have already met this method of interpretation in the work of Justin and Clement; the method as such was no novelty in the Church. But because of the reflective thoroughness with which Origen handles it, it now assumes an all-embracing theological significance. To our way of thinking it thereby becomes quite fantastic, but it is of the essence of allegory that the more uncompromisingly and consistently it is applied the more it seems to be justified and confirmed. Its results can no more be contradicted than the presuppositions on which it is based can be checked by the actual text.

Origen was therefore in no doubt that his procedure was methodical, perfectly scientific, and appropriate. As we have said, he was able to refer to the theories of Hellenistic philology, and for him the allegorical method is justified above all because it is sometimes used even in the Bible. With its spiritual relativity and gradations, it fits in marvellously with his whole outlook. It should therefore not surprise us that he was quite convinced of the validity of his insights.

For every text in the Bible Origen distinguishes between a physical (or material), a psychic, and a spiritual meaning. This corresponds roughly, though not entirely, with the later distinction between historical, moral, and theological meaning. Normally, however, the two higher levels coincide and the first, the physical or historical interpretation, is sometimes left out altogether. In Origen's view there are texts which it would be quite absurd and immoral to interpret literally. They are intended, through the offence they give, to point to the real, deeper meaning which lies below the surface of the text. 'What reasonable person will believe for example that the first, second, and third day, evening and morning, came into being without the sun, moon, and stars, and the first day even without the sky?' Or 'Who would not be led to regard unchastity as nothing, when he reads how Judah lay down with a harlot or the patriarchs had several wives simultaneously?' (*De Princ.* IV, 16) —unless all these things are only taken figuratively, as it is proper that they should be, and affirmed in their true spiritual sense. Otherwise a Christian would have to blush for the divine law of the Old Testament in view of the 'much finer and more sensible laws of the Romans or Athenians' for instance (*Hom. Lev.* 5, 1). Such considerations make it clear that the moralizing, rationalistic, and unhistorical conception of the Bible forces Origen to accept allegory as a way out. It was impossible to defend the Old Testament against the pagans and above all against the criticisms of the Gnostic and Marcionite heretics in any other way. It must also be admitted that in spite of the essential wrongness of the method, the allegorical interpretation does not necessarily always miss the point at issue in the Bible. In the course of the Church's history it has often been the means of arriving at the true meaning of the text, albeit in a roundabout way. This is, however, seldom the case in Origen. It is deeply moving to note with what energy and earnestness this great and devout scholar dedicates the work of a lifetime to fathoming the truth of this one ardently loved book, firmly convinced that he is on the way to penetrating ever more deeply into its content, while in fact he remains the prisoner of the assumptions of his Platonizing and Gnosticizing outlook, incapable even of seeing what separates him from the Old and New Testaments.

None of those who fell under his spell fared any differently, and their numbers grew rapidly. Origen was by nature no solitary scholar, but primarily a teacher who devoted himself, like Clement, but with far greater thoroughness, to the oral instruction and tuition of his pupils. We still have the valedictory address of one of them, Gregory Thaumaturgus ('wonder-worker'), who later became an equally famous bishop and missionary in Asia Minor. In this address he expressed his enthusiastic thanks to his beloved teacher. For him Origen was the only man he knows who 'understands the divine utterances purely and clearly and knows how to interpret them to others' (Greg. Thaumat. XV, 175). Under the guidance of this teacher, he says, nothing had remained 'hidden and inaccessible'. Origen knew the right answer to every question and set every fact in its right place. Through a well-to-do patron called Ambrosius, whom he had himself converted previously from heresy to the Catholic truth, abundant resources for scholarly work and publication had been made available to him. 'Seven stenographers who relieved one another at definite intervals, and just as many book scribes and female calligraphers' (Eus. *H.E.* VI, 23, 2), were always available and saw to it that as far as possible not a word of his was lost.

The almost incredible productivity of this man, who, according to his own testimony, had never known a moment's rest throughout his life and acquired the somewhat ambiguous nickname of the 'worker with brazen bowels' (Chalkenteros), can only be explained if we bear all this secretarial help in mind. Nearly all his writings bear the marks of unpolished oral delivery. But they were read throughout the Greek-speaking Church, far beyond the confines of Alexandria and his own school.

Meanwhile Origen had become a world celebrity. The pagan Governor of Arabia appealed to his Egyptian colleague and also wrote to Bishop Demetrius a courteous letter asking for Origen to be allowed to give a few lectures in his presence. On the orders of the Empress Julia Mammaea he was escorted to her court at Antioch because she wished to receive 'a sample of his universally admired insight into divine things' (Eus. *H.E.* VI, 21, 3). There also existed letters from a later period which Origen had sent to the Emperor Philip the Arab and his wife, who were favourably disposed toward the Christians. Within the Church itself Origen was naturally regarded even more as an authority. He received invitations from all quarters, and he was

called in to help especially when it was a case of refuting a
learned heretic or clarifying difficult theological problems.
Origen not only knew how to impress his opponents by his
learning and sagacity but also how to convince them inwardly
and win them for the Catholic Church. The recently discovered
proceedings of one such disputation which the whole congregation attended give a vivid picture of his bearing as modest as
it was distinguished, and his thoroughly objective method of
attack.

At first sight it seems astonishing that this man became involved more and more in ecclesiastic differences and difficulties
in his immediate homeland, which were ultimately to lead to
open conflict. The 'case of Origen' is the first celebrated example of rivalry and conflict between the free, unofficial power
of an independent 'teacher' and the authority of his ecclesiastical superiors. It is no longer possible to unravel all the details
of the dispute. Besides personal disagreements, doubt regarding
his orthodoxy may have played a part from the outset. The
decisive factor, however, was probably the question of the legal
position of the school of Origen in relation to the doctrinal
authority of the 'apostolic' bishop. Demetrius was a determined
hierarch who was already making a successful effort to gain
recognition for his authority throughout Egypt. He wanted to
bring the 'catechetical school' also under his immediate super-
vision; but here he met with opposition. One recalls the carefree nonchalance with which, a generation earlier, Clement of
Alexandria had fashioned his theological teaching. It had not
occurred to him to refer to clerical authority, nor was there any
need for him to do so in view of his completely independent
position. Origen was more ecclesiastically-minded from the
very outset. He wanted to serve the whole Church as a teacher
and at the same time be a loyal member of his own Alexandrian
Church. He too regarded himself, however, as free to teach
what he thought fit, and not subject to any human judgment,
willing though he was to face any criticism and questions. God
himself had blessed him, like an early Christian prophet, with

the gift of wisdom and a knowledge of the Scriptures which, by their very nature, were reserved to the few. It is true that Origen had no desire to upset the Christian faith of the simple Church member and warmly acknowledged the value of simple faith. But the higher knowledge still had rights of its own and ought not to be measured by the normal standards of the average Christian. Origen was striving to combine and hold in balance the different degrees of spiritual maturity and illumination, but this only draws attention to the mental reservations and superiority of the 'Gnostics'; the difference cannot be overlooked and the suspicions of the 'simple' were aroused. This was the situation that faced the bishop. Origen tried to overcome the threatening breach by purely spiritual means, pointing to the substantial orthodoxy of his 'higher' theology and his willingness to share in the life and worship of the Church. But Demetrius required formal integration and submission legally and in practice: the God-ordained, monarchic episcopacy was to be the living guarantee of orthodox truth and the clear and sole expression of Church unity.

In Origen's view the simplest solution of the tense situation would have been to ordain him to the priesthood and combine his official and unofficial authority in a kind of personal unity. It seems that he made efforts to this end, but in vain. Demetrius wanted submission to himself, and in view of the almost episcopal standing of the Alexandrian presbyters the independence of the head of the school would only have been increased if he had also been ordained. Outside Egypt no one understood the way ecclesiastic politics was run in Egypt. In Jerusalem, whose bishop had been friendly with Clement of Alexandria, in Caesarea, where a pupil of Origen's was at the head of the Church, he was allowed to preach in church without any question. The violent protests which Demetrius made against this 'unheard-of' innovation were rejected. But when some years later Origen was staying in Palestine again, on his way to Greece on Church business, it was suddenly decided to ordain him to the priesthood. Origen made no objection, clearly hoping that he would now be free from further restrictions on his activities. But the opposite happened. The move made his position in Alexandria quite untenable. On his return home he was given such an unfriendly reception that he was forced to the decision to abandon altogether his field of activity at home and move to Caesarea, where he was received with open arms. At a synod of priests held in Alexandria, Demetrius had him formally banished, and in the year 231–32 a second synod deposed him from the priesthood because it had been conferred on him without reference to the proper authority and was in any case illegal since he was a eunuch.

This apparently fortuitous, arbitrarily provoked conflict points to a deeper antithesis of which the immediate participants were probably not completely aware at the time. It is clear that for all his love of peace and personal humility, Origen could not concede to the office of bishop the importance which was claimed for it, and that for reasons of theological and religious principle. In his opinion, the thing that matters in the long run, the living knowledge of the truth, cannot be transmitted and controlled by officials. All the rights which the bishop is accorded and possesses, the sacraments which he administers, the power of excommunication and absolution which he exerts, remain purely external so long as they are not impregnated with real spiritual power. This cannot be effected by the office as such but only by the Holy Spirit, by the right attitude of love and the knowledge which God gives and which the spiritual teacher above all communicates. Origen's views are not in the least revolutionary. He knows and gladly emphasizes that Christendom must, like every 'people', have its rulers and that order in the Church is absolutely necessary. For this reason alone office-bearers deserve obedience and respect, and Origen desires with his whole heart that they should all be enlightened to the greatest possible extent with spiritual gifts and be real teachers and patterns to their flocks. But he also knows and sees just as clearly that that is all too often just what they fail to be, and the spiritual man is in principle free and independent of their authority. With one half of his nature Origen is a conservative, ecclesiastical pietist; but with the other half he remains a liberal idealist who at heart lives more in the invisible than in the visible Church. He was the first for whom this momentous distinction came to assume fundamental theological importance.

He bore with calm dignity 'all the winds of malice' (*Comm. Joh.* VI, prol. 9) which Demetrius now let loose against his former protégé. By concentrating on his theological work he tried to overcome his bitterness, and he consoled himself with the remembrance of the Biblical saying that no one should trust in man. His enemies were, he thought, more to be pitied than hated. One should pray for them, not curse them, since we have been created to bless. Outwardly Demetrius was unable to do him any further harm. He tried in vain to stir up his episcopal colleagues outside Egypt against Origen. The school was re-established in Caesarea. Origen also laboured eagerly as a preacher to the congregation. His pupils and episcopal friends loved and revered him as a saint. It was in Caesarea that Origen finally secured the supreme glory known to the Church: suffering unto death for the truth of his Faith and his Lord.

The major part of Origen's life fell in a period of 'peace', a period of calm, sometimes even friendly understanding between the State and the Church. As a good Platonist Origen showed much appreciation for the rights of rulers and the responsibility which every citizen is called to bear for the welfare of the State. But a cheap syncretism and political compromise were equally alien to his mind. Christians were different from all the other peoples contained in the Roman Empire inasmuch as they were the holy people of God, who do not interfere in the affairs of the world and can never be made subservient to its aims. Christians fulfil their external duties and also pray for the Emperor and his army, but they must refuse to bear arms themselves since they are a priestly race, recognizing only the warfare of the spirit. In his old age Origen wrote an elaborate *Apology* in which he tried to refute the criticisms

which the pagan philosopher Celsus had made of Christians two
generations ago. Once again his two sides come out: the close
affinity of outlook with his philosophical opponent and his
proud sense of superiority as a Christian. Soon afterwards, with
the accession of the new Emperor Decius in the year 249, a
political change occurred and the first systematic persecution of
the Christians to cover the whole Empire was launched.

It was no longer feasible to destroy the Church by direct
physical extermination of its individual members. It was a
matter of forcing them to surrender by terrorism and well-
conceived measures of coercion, and the first and most important step was the subjugation or removal of their leaders.
Origen, who was now an old man of nearly seventy, was
arrested, cast into prison, and cruelly tortured. It was clearly
not intended to kill him, but he was put to the rack and his feet
stretched for days on end 'as far as the fourth hole'. He was
threatened with death by burning, but for all this nothing was
achieved. Origen had to be released, but he was physically
broken. Nevertheless he wrote a few more short treatises
'which were of great use to those in need of consolation' (Eus.
H.E. VI, 39, 5). He died at the latest in the year 254.

To the very end the picture presented by the life and character of this strange man was remarkably clear and consistent.
Austere and yet kind, wholly pure and honest, entirely dedicated to intellectual work and ascetic piety, he was a scholar
and above all a systematic thinker, capable of taking on any
opponent. He was in no sense a problematical character nor in
the final analysis an original one. He combined the unphilosophical tradition of the Church with the Gnostic-Neoplatonic
tendencies of the century on a higher intellectual plane and thus
created a theological structure of admirable grandeur and completeness. But he had no feeling for the deeper, essential problems of a truly Christian theology. For that very reason his
solutions met with an easy and apparently uncontroversial success. They were the solutions of a theorist of genius who constructed reality from the idea, without being moved at a deeper

level by doubt and suffering. Such people do not find it difficult to obtain pupils and successors. It was only among the succeeding generations of his followers that the progress of historical development brought to light slowly but surely the spiritual inadequacies of the theology of Origen. The new generation confronted this development all the more helplessly because it was unable to refer to its revered master for guidance for its troubles and problems, while it knew at the same time that it was his inferior in systematic power and discipline of thought, in universality and thoroughness of philosophical culture, and in purity of intention and conviction.

CHAPTER V

EUSEBIUS OF CAESAREA

HALF a century after the death of Origen his theology had spread throughout the Eastern Church. It was regarded as the only really scientific theology in harmony with higher and, in particular, philosophical culture. The literary champions of Christianity, the intellectually active, working Christians at the schools and training centres, the bishops of the larger sees, adhered to it and strove to teach and act in its spirit. Imperceptibly the tradition began to change, to become mingled with other traditions, and to adapt itself to new situations in the Church and the world of ideas. As these changes took place, intellectual divisions arose and inner weaknesses became apparent, which were the less easily overcome because it was no longer possible consistently to maintain Origen's philosophical assumptions. Aristotelian concepts and ideas were altering the Platonic foundations of the system, ecclesiastical interests and consideration for the literal truth of the Bible were demanding their rights, and new problems were coming to the fore.

Origen had been a systematic thinker, and as such he had shaped his exegesis and his theology and ontology into a single, unifying pattern. The new generation of theologians tried to use new methods. The change-over from philosophy to philology, to the critically exact examination of the biblical foundations, is discernible in the personality and work of Pamphilus. Pamphilus was a wealthy lawyer from Berytus, in Phoenicia, who decided, under the influence of Pierius, the director of the catechetical school in Alexandria, to abandon his public career and devote his whole life to the service of the Church. As presbyter of the church in Caesarea he became the librarian in charge of Origen's literary estate, which he began to sort and sift. Above all, he endeavoured to produce a reliable text of the Bible on the basis of the *Hexapla* and Origen's commentaries on the Old and New Testaments. In this task he required assistants and collaborators, and the young Eusebius became the most useful and industrious member of his team. He helped Eusebius to achieve economic and intellectual independence, and Eusebius, who owed everything to him for his start, expressed his attachment by combining, in the manner of a liberated slave, his master's name with his own. Thus, he entered literature and the history of the Church as 'Eusebius Pamphili'. There is still extant a manuscript of the Bible with a note recording their joint work of revision. Eusebius took over from his master a profound veneration for Origen and occupied himself with his literary remains in order still further to enhance the reputation of the incomparable teacher. He tried to produce a complete corpus of Origen's correspondence which was intended to prevent its dispersion and the disintegration of the tradition. During the last great persecution Pamphilus was cast into prison, and in the face of death he decided to write another *Apology* for the great teacher which was intended to protect him from the criticisms levelled at Origen by his fellow-prisoners and various recent theologians. This was Pamphilus's only independent piece of writing and at the same time the first production of his pupil Eusebius, who assisted him and had to finish it independently. Pamphilus died a martyr; Eusebius, who was still unknown at the time, escaped with his life. His fame as a scholar was soon to outshine that of his master.

First of all, Eusebius continued his academic studies indefatigably in spite of the storms of continuing persecution, and he collected like an archivist all the information about martyrdoms and other events in the Church that he could lay his hands on. He then came forward with writings of his own. Apart from purely philosophical, historical, and exegetical researches, they consist mainly of a number of comprehensive tracts directed against the pagan and Jewish opponents of Christianity.

Eusebius was a believing Christian and felt most deeply an obligation to help the cause of the Faith and the Church with his learning and gifts. From the year 313 the Church had again acquired the freedom to develop without hindrance and appeared to be moving into a new and finer future.

If one compares the early theological works of this period with the works of the earlier apologists like Justin, the difference in the situation and the personal quality of Eusebius at once become apparent. Christendom was no longer the poor little band of 'barbaric' sectaries which had to struggle laboriously for its right to exist and enjoy a modicum of intellectual respect in a rich, self-assured world. It had long since spread through the entire civilized world; cities and countrysides were influenced by its churches, and in all professions and not least the intellectual the activity of Christians had grown to immense proportions. Whereas pagan society had become impoverished and morally degenerate at the time of the civil wars and universal decline, thanks to its firm coherence, discipline, and the unbroken courage of its Faith the Church had maintained itself and continued to grow uninterruptedly. Thus it now appeared in a different light. For Eusebius the apologetic evidence for the truth of Christianity no longer depended on certain miraculous details and correspondences which relate the prophecies of the Old Testament to Christ. The victory of the true monotheistic knowledge of God, the new life of virtue which had come to life in the Church, the expansion and visible triumph of the Church 'among all peoples'—all these things speak for themselves. It is merely a matter of demonstrating that this whole astonishing development lay in God's plan from the beginning and could only have been brought to the brink of fulfilment by the wonderful aid of God himself. Paganism, with its polytheism and blood sacrifices, its demonic superstition and the everlastingly fruitless conflict of its philosophies, now seems like an outdated form of religion which must and will disappear. It can no longer hold its own in the forum of enlightened reason and a higher morality.

The change in the situation also brought a shift of emphasis
in the meaning of the Christian hope. It was no longer centred
exclusively in the world to come: it began to be realized in the
present world. Christianity was the decisive power behind the
moral progress of the world, the crowning consummation of
the history of thought and religion, and its prophecies and
commandments had become the bases of a programme of
human renewal. Monotheism and the new idealistic morality,
which constituted the heart of the gospel of Jesus for Eusebius,
were unable to rule the world from the beginning. First of all,
the nomadic stage of civilization had to be overcome; cities had
to be built, laws made, arts and skills developed, and 'life, which
was still to some extent animal and unworthy', had to be tamed
and moulded by the beginnings of philosophy and civilization
(*H.E.* I, 2, 17-19). When the Roman Empire brought peace to
the world and overcame the multiplicity of governments, the
hour for the international and peaceable Christian race had
come, according to the will of God (*Praep. Ev.* I, 4). To begin
with, they remained with their claims half in the background,
in order not to provoke the Roman rulers and disturb the peace
of the Empire; now, however, in the age of fulfilment Christians had become the open and natural allies of the secular
power. This is an idea that had long been latent in the conception of Christianity as the consummation of ancient philosophy
and culture. The beginnings of Eusebius's conception are to be
found in Origen, especially where he contends with the pagan
enemies of the Church. But fundamentally his frame of mind
was far too otherworldly and dualistic seriously to pursue such
ideas.

Origen was not interested in world history and politics. The
victory of the Church was for him perhaps an idea which might
be considered theoretically but it was not yet a goal to which
all one's energies could or should be bent. Eusebius's attitude
was quite different. It is true that for him too God himself was
a completely transcendent reality, and he regarded pure, ascetic
withdrawal from the world and the worship of the divine

Being as the supreme goal of Christian piety. The celibate priests of the Church, its holy, spiritual top layer of leaders, must satisfy in a representative capacity this demand. But with this representative service, the claims of the world-renouncing ideal have been essentially met. It is beyond the scope of a 'universal, human way of life' and must therefore remain the exception to the rule. The majority of Christians have their tasks within this world, yet in spite of that they have their full share of salvation and the saving teaching of the Church (*Demonstr. Ev.* I, 8, 29 f.). God has protected his Church in the world from all the demonic onslaughts of its enemies 'plainly from on high' and has led it to victory and success as a light to lighten the nations.

Such are the ideas that made Eusebius a Church historian. Early Church history grew out of apologetics just as modern history grew out of the Enlightenment. That is the reason for the inner weakness of Eusebius's position. His works on Church history and contemporary history favour a moralizing, black-and-white technique because their intentions are apologetic; he has a fondness for the rhetorical and the edifying and strives all the time to impress and convince the reader. He is lacking in strict theological criteria. Of course it is God who achieves the Church's successes, and they are all miraculous; its defeats are the work of the demonic powers and the human villains who are their accomplices. But they can also be imposed by God to test or punish the Church. They are in no case the last word; even within the Church the apostolic truth will always win in the long run against all heretical innovations. The old mythological framework, which reckoned the history of the world according to Daniel's 'weeks of years' and ended with the return of Christ at a date which can be calculated, was abandoned by Eusebius once and for all; the optimistic scheme of a progressive, God-guided education of the human race is the basis of his whole view of the world and the plan of salvation. Beyond that he was not interested in the fundamental problems of a theology of history, and for that reason his critical sense and his interest in the materials of history were able to develop without restraint.

In this respect his work was exemplary for its period and deserves all praise. Eusebius was really a scholar, and the conscientiousness and precision of his philological, archaeological, and historical researches are apparent wherever we are able to test them. But for him we should know about as much of the first centuries of the Church's history as we should know of early Christianity if Luke had not written the Acts of the Apostles. In contrast to the latter work, Eusebius's *History of the Church* is, admittedly, by no means a work of art. The multifarious material is laid out in columns rather than worked up into a definite shape. For pages on end quotations are allowed to break into the exposition and the overwhelmingly vigorous style pours over us in a torrent of solemn-sounding, hardly intelligible words and phrases. Yet in his own time Eusebius was esteemed as an orator. His reputation as a scholar may have influenced this judgment of him.

Even before he began his *History of the Church* Eusebius had worked out his 'chronological tables' on the model of the earlier Christian chroniclers, though more thoroughly and in greater detail. After a long and learned introduction about the different chronological systems he presents synchronistic tables of the history of the world. The juxtaposition of Biblical and secular dates was intended to prove that Christianity, far from being a recent religion, was, with its Old Testament witnesses, the oldest and most venerable religion in the world. Christ brought in its final period, which was now unfolding itself in the history of the Church. From this point on, the material in the column devoted to the plan of salvation becomes larger and larger, almost crowding out the secular records. The *History of the Church* is to some extent an independent version of this part of the chronicle, issued as a new book. The rather external manner in which it sets information about famous bishops, theologians, heries, persecutions, the destinies of the Jewish people, and other matters side by side still shows the influence of the earlier method. Nevertheless, Eusebius rightly stressed the novelty of his undertaking and the special difficulties presented by a first attempt of this kind. He regarded himself as treading a completely new path 'without finding the slightest trace of men who have trod it before me, only occasional minute records in which one man in one way, another in another left behind a fragmentary account of his own time' (*H.E.* I, 1, 3). These earlier records must give him his direction, like beacons or distant calls in the dark. As we have said, Eusebius was fond of quoting such records verbatim, especially when they seemed to have chronological value, and in this way numerous fragments of a literature have been preserved which would otherwise have been completely lost. Seen as a whole, Eusebius did his work so thoroughly that it remained authoritative for a long time. The Church historians of the following century merely continued or simply translated this basic work.

Eusebius's exposition begins with Jesus Christ, whose nature and activities 'present themselves to a conscientious investigator so sublimely and so powerfully that they can no longer be human' (*H.E.* I, 1, 7). He then leads up in seven books to his own immediate period, and he deals with this in the last three books. Even today it is possible to see that Eusebius did not write these parts all at once but continually worked at them and improved them, as further developments took place and new information reached him.

His judgment on the rulers varies according to the measure of their success and their changing attitude to Christianity. The author's personal bias and propagandist intentions now become very pronounced and cast a dubious light on his often mutually contradictory reports. In the final edition the work achieved its manifest consummation; history itself supplied the historian of the Church Triumphant with the appropriate conclusion. The victory of the Emperor Constantine, friend of Christians and beloved of God, and the beginning of his sole reign in East and West alike (324), brought the previous development to its goal and a new epoch opened. For Eusebius too a new era began in his own life. Up till then Eusebius had not been a public man or a Church politician. He was a scholar with heart and soul and as a theologian a champion of the truth and the rights of the Christian Church. Like Origen, he held the position of a presbyter in Caesarea, and in 313–14 this accomplished and cultured priest was made bishop of that city. As a cleric he no doubt fulfilled his duties according to rule; but fundamentally he remained the man he really was, devoted above all to his scholarly labours. He was not a teacher like Origen; he was primarily a research worker, a historian, a philologist, and an apologist. He also preached much less often than Origen, in spite of the acknowledged and representative position he had gained in the Church. This was not due to indifference toward the duties of his office and spiritual calling. We have seen that he put his whole work, including his strictly academic studies, at the service of the Church, and he now thought he discerned entirely new opportunities for service. With the victory of Constantine the Church emerged from the period of preparation into the age of fulfilment. 'These things were foretold by Isaiah and laid down in Holy Scripture from time immemorial; the infallibility of these oracles now had to be proved by deeds' (H.E. X, 4, 53). The political victor becomes the bringer of salvation to the world.

Eusebius had stressed the providentially intimate relationship between the Empire and the Church on an earlier occasion; he now included the institution of emperorship and the person of the Emperor in this relationship. The Emperor sent by God, the redeemer who appears after the long torment of dissension and persecution, is God's chosen herald for the whole world. His earthly dominion is the image of the rule of God and the rule of Christ which the Bible foretold. The final order of things had now been achieved. 'God himself, the Great King, stretched forth his right hand from above and made him to this day victor over all his haters and enemies' (Laus Const. 8). This Emperor, beloved of God, is a philosopher and a pattern of all piety, the essence of all kingly virtues, dignity, beauty, and strength, culture, inborn reason, and divine wisdom. Eusebius claims that he had realized this many years ago when he saw the then quite unknown prince for the first time.

Eusebius has often been criticized for the extravagance of such utterances and the insincerity of his 'Byzantinism'. But it is easy to forget the degree to which such expressions had come to be taken for granted in the Orientalized court style of the time. Moreover, Constantine knew how to handle people. He obviously attached importance to the support of the distinguished scholar and his propaganda for the Church, and met him with due deference and the most flattering regard. Eusebius was a man of lowly origin, by no means at home in the great world of politics, and it is not surprising that he allowed himself to be hoodwinked. The important thing, however, was his realization of the basic agreement which bound him to the Emperor with a kind of theological inevitability. This rationalistic philosopher and apostle of the new Christian order was inevitably a 'Byzantine Christian'. His whole theology was aimed at fulfilment in a moral civilization united to a world church. Unknown to himself, it became the up-to-date Christian version of the old pagan ideology of Empire and Emperor. Eusebius would have had to surrender his own self if he had not at this moment followed the Emperor as the 'chosen instrument' of God for whom he had hoped and in whose mission and destiny he believed. For him a final 'victory' for the Church could be conceived only in alliance with the Empire and only under the auspices of the permanent unity of a Christian order and a holy, world-wide peace which it was the task of the Emperor to create and preserve.

This was Eusebius's Christianity, and it led to his ruin as an ecclesiastical politician. The Arian controversy was dividing the Greek Church at the very moment of Constantine's victory. Fundamentally, it had nothing at all to do with politics, but it could not have come at a more awkward moment. It was essentially a struggle for the bases of the Christian belief in salvation, which had its origin and foundation in the divine and human person of Christ. Eusebius was by no means the convinced 'Arian' which he has been alleged to be by historians of heresy. Christ was for him more than a mere creature and more than a superior demigod. Arius, whom Eusebius had taken in as a refugee, had cleverly, but rather deceitfully, misled him to begin with as to the radicalism of his Christology. Eusebius was persuaded to see in the exile an innocent victim of persecution who had, like Origen, come to Caesarea because the power-loving Alexandrian patriarch refused to permit the development of a scientific theology. Old errors about the complete identity of the Father with the Son, which had long since been refuted by Origen, appeared to be coming up again in the camp of the enemies of Arius. For Eusebius their massive confessions of faith meant the end of an up-to-date, philosophically grounded and scientifically defensible theology. He therefore became a convinced supporter of Arius. But fundamentally he was not interested in the 'mystery of human redemption' as such; he was fighting rather for the intellectual and moral aspirations which the Church's monotheistic preaching now had to uphold in the new world order. Against this background, the Christological disputes seemed like mere quibbles, or at any rate they were not entitled to a place in the foreground of ecclesiastical politics as his opponents desired. With genuine horror Eusebius noted how in the historical hour of liberation and God-given victory theological quarrelsomeness and intolerance threatened to shatter the relationship of the Empire and the Church and the united Christian front was breaking up 'so that the holy mysteries of the divine teachings suffer shameful derision in the very midst of the theatres of unbelievers' (*Vit. Const.* II, 61). On this point there was a genuine unanimity between himself and Constantine. They both had the same goal in view: to overcome this unpleasant situation as quickly as possible, cost what it might. Only Eusebius was also a theologian and bishop of his Church. By half unconsciously making tactical and political ends the criterion of his decisions he involved himself in contradictions which landed him in personal humiliation and forced him, despite his honest intentions, to take steps which irreparably compromised his reputation. At the Council of Nicaea (325) Constantine was compelled to yield to the opponents of Arius. Even Eusebius must now have come to realize how dubious the Arian teaching was. Nevertheless, he strove to remain loyal to his protégé. In the end, however, he had to drop him in order to save himself from ex-communication and deposal. The mediating confession of faith which he submitted to the Council was publicly praised by Constantine but modified so extensively by all kind of anti-Arian additions that Eusebius himself could no longer have honestly accepted it. He was nevertheless forced to sign it, and the tortuous letter in which he justified his action to his own church proves, with its untenable reinterpretations and evasions, that he knew perfectly well what he had done. Nor was this the end of his dishonesty. In favour with the Emperor once again and deemed worthy of intimate intercourse with him, he used his influence to get the decision that had been taken reversed by indirect ways in striking a personal blow at the supporters of the Nicene Creed and giving his enthusiastic assent to their dismissal and banishment by political means.

We do not need to study the events in detail. Needless to say, the theological treatises which Eusebius wrote still reached a high intellectual level even though they were inspired by personal annoyance. He also continued his scholarly researches, and he was regarded as the leading spokesman of the Church, an outstanding champion of the imperial policy for Church and State in the new era. His supreme triumph was when Constantine had him appointed bishop of the bitterly contested see of Antioch. Eusebius modestly declined the appointment on the ground that his acceptance would infringe certain ecclesiastical statutes. Perhaps he sensed his own limitations. Anyway, he preferred to stay with his incomparable library in Caesarea, amidst his familiar surroundings. He died there peacefully a few years after Constantine (339–40).

In the end Eusebius was able to believe that he had attained the goal of his life's work. State and Church had come together; the 'peace' of a unity based on political foundations seemed to be firmly established; a middle-of-the-road theology, such as appealed to him, dominated the field. And yet this impression was based on an illusion. In the very next generation the opposition to the régime in power, which had been officially reduced to silence, was to emerge again with renewed passion and compel a basic revision of all the decisions which Eusebius and his friends had secured on tactical and political rather than dogmatic and ecclesiastical grounds. Later on, the Church decided more or less firmly that Eusebius could not be regarded as orthodox and saw in him a 'double-faced' man (Socr. *H.E.* I, 23) even though it could not dispense with his historical and philological works 'for the sake of the factual information which is useful for instruction' (*Decr. Gelas.* 5, 22). In this it has been less than just to his qualities as a man. His destiny reveals more than the personal failure of an otherwise respectable scholar who was not equal to the difficulties of imperial and ecclesiastical politics which confronted him. It reveals more the bankruptcy of a theological trend which was unable, for political reasons, to free itself from the power and opportunities of the moment and could not take itself or its faith in Christ really seriously. The crisis of Origenism thus became evident and made a new understanding of the Church's teaching urgently necessary. This was bound to have an effect on the position of responsible theologians and teachers.

CHAPTER VI

ATHANASIUS

ATHANASIUS belongs to a much younger generation than Eusebius. He was born *circa* 295, and his memories did not go back earlier than the last persecutions. These he did experience, however, and the hardness of his character, his mania for absolute, cut and dried decisions, may have been increased by these early experiences. As a young man, however, Athanasius grew up within the order of the Imperial Church: this was an accepted institution to which he held fast throughout his life. But with him a new era begins in theology too. Athanasius was the first Greek Father of the Church who was not at home in the academic atmosphere of Christian philosophy. He was a 'Churchman' who was also well-versed in theological matters, but he was trained in the administration of the Alexandrian hierarchy. His spiritual home was the divine service and the administrative desk in the ecclesiastical office, not the school platform. At the beginning of the third century no bishop possessed such a large, well-organized, and efficient administrative machine as the Patriarch of Alexandria. From the time of Bishop Demetrius, who died in 232, ecclesiastically Alexandria dominated the whole of Egypt and also the adjacent areas of Libya and the Pentapolis. He had appointed the first bishops in his province, and they remained dependent on him and he had taken up the cudgels with heretics and other recalcitrant elements. We have already encountered Demetrius as the opponent of Origen. But theology had not died out in Alexandria since his banishment. Bishop Dionysius 'the Great' (who died in 265) had been a pupil of Origen and was also well known as a theologian. But just as the catechetical school had

lost its old independence, so theology now had to take into
account the practical demands of Church life and Church politics. One senses this in the very beginnings of the Arian controversy. For the new Bishop Alexander the main thing was to
force the refractory presbyter Arius to submit to the official
discipline of his spiritual superior. Furthermore, the earlier
Egyptian schism caused by the breakaway of the supporters of
Melitius, whom Arius had joined for a time, became mixed up
with the theological controversy. From the very outset the
dogmatic problem became in Egypt a problem of episcopal
authority and the 'church law'.

Athanasius became familiar with this whole world of ecclesiastical politics and administrative problems perhaps while he
was still half a boy. He was reader, then deacon and as such the
special confidant and theological adviser of his bishop, whom
he was allowed to accompany to the Council of Nicaea. When
Alexander died in 328, he is said to have wanted Athanasius to
succeed him. His rapid election was not carried through without opposition. Perhaps people were afraid of the ruthless
energy of this unusually young but no longer unknown candidate. His opposition to the Arians was certain. He also sought
to take immediate and brutally decisive action against the
Melitians, with whom negotiations were still in progress, with
the result that their resistance flared up again. But Athanasius
would undoubtedly have coped with these domestic problems.
The important thing was that the Arian controversy had long
since extended beyond the vicinity of Egypt itself and had
penetrated the whole of the East. By taking up the attack again
with renewed vigour Athanasius once again called into question the almost complete victory of the opposition party. From
now on the struggle was never to let him go nor he to let it go.
For forty-five years he continued to wage it with unvarying
tenacity, agility, and energy, showing versatility in his methods
and formulations, unshaken and relentless on the essential issues,
reassured by no partial success, and discouraged by no failures.
When Athanasius died, he stood on the brink of victory. The

whole subsequent development of the Greek-Byzantine Imperial Church was based on the struggle and success of this one man.

The decision of Nicaea was no accident; but the way it was brought about was essentially the result of tactical measures and pressure on the part of the Emperor. What Constantine was worried about above all was the pacification and firm unification of the Imperial Church he had founded. The condemnation of Arius and the Nicene Creed were both intended to serve this end. When complete success was not achieved the Emperor was, as we have seen, persuaded by his advisers to extend the limits of comprehension in the universal Church somewhat further, and he subsequently revoked the decision that had been made. Finally Arius was taken into favour. The formal order to recognize this decision in Alexandria and to admit the condemned heretic to his old sphere of activity for the sake of 'harmony' arrived there just as Alexander was dying. He died before he could answer the Emperor's communication. It fell to his successor to make the decision.

Athanasius was not in doubt for a moment about what should be done. To restore Arius would be out of the question. Whatever explanation he might have given, such a step would be taken by the public only as implying a withdrawal and as a theological and political defeat of the Alexandrian bishop from which his opponents alone would have benefited. Athanasius took the position that the admission of people 'who had invented a heresy in opposition to the truth and had been anathematized by a general synod' was fundamentally impossible (*Apol.* II, 59, 5). To expect Arius seriously to change his mind was also out of the question, and Athanasius was therefore able to consider himself in the right not only on tactical grounds. Unlike Alexander, he had realized the scope and significance of the theological conflict from the outset. The Arian doctrine of 'createdness', that is, the no longer essentially divine nature of the Redeemer, was for him not the questionable or perverse solution of a theological problem but the end of the Christian

Faith itself, the betrayal of everything the Church had been concerned with from the very beginning. Athanasius did not regard the wider theological and political ideals to which Eusebius had so ably devoted himself in the struggle for his rationalist and relativist Christology of any importance. The Church is not concerned with any secular programme, but with man's eternal salvation. The world of the created and man's much-praised reason had obviously not been able to save him from corruption. It needed the coming of Christ 'the Logos, who was the Logos through himself' (*Contra Gentes* 40); he had to take our flesh and thus unite our nature with God and God's eternal life. The Incarnation was the decisive event in the process of salvation. God himself acted by pulling down the barrier to his fallen creature and bringing to light life and immortality, with the knowledge of his true nature. A demi-god would have been of no use to man. The moral aspect of the process of Redemption, the idea of the knowledge of sin, of atonement, and the forgiveness of sins, are of only secondary interest to Athanasius. Salvation from death and the life-giving fellowship with God are central. With genuine religious fervour he acclaims the miracle of Christ's coming. This is a theology that has little in common with Origen in any shape or form. Athanasius naturally knew 'the supremely learned and diligent Origen' and occasionally tried to defend him from an allegedly improper 'Arian' interpretation (*De Decr.* 27, 1; *Ad Serap.* 4, 9); but on the whole he mentions him very seldom. He reminds us most of all of the emotional faith of the aged Irenaeus.

According to Athanasius, the whole Church can live only on the one truth of the true God and Saviour Jesus Christ, which is proclaimed in the preaching of the Church and represented miraculously and effectively in its sacraments. Whoever does not believe and feel this truth, whoever is satisfied with general theories of virtue and pale speculations about the spirit, the world, and a creaturely Logos-Christ, is an 'Arian', though he deny it a thousand times over. There is something almost monomaniacal about the monotonous regularity with which Athanasius rams home the same basic ideas and harks back incessantly to the same complaints and accusations. But it would be wrong to suspect stupidity or theological incompetence behind this highly effective method. Athanasius knew how to organize his material clearly and shrewdly; in the development of his ideas he shows a striking dialectical skill and art, and his Biblical exegesis, which has to carry the dogmatic proof, is often discerning and profound, for all its violence. It is obvious that he had been a good student in his youth and is a well-trained theologian. But it is difficult to feel that theological work as such gave him any pleasure, let alone that he had any desire to make use of it for the purpose of educating others or set himself up as a 'teacher'. For him theology was simply a weapon. Athanasius's writings were devoted almost entirely to controversy. There is an occasional note of mistrust in Hellenistic culture; at any rate, he completely ignores its treasures. As a person he naturally thought of himself as a Greek. But it is hardly an accident that he was, as we know, the first theologian of any standing to preach in Coptic. There was something un-Greek about his nature, which is harsh and rigid, without a touch of intellectual grace or charm. His portrait, if we possessed one, would probably recall the ancient Pharaohs and their officials more than a Greek philosopher.

Even before Constantine was able to return to the case of Arius, further complaints had been lodged against Athanasius by the Melitians. He was alleged to have bribed an imperial messenger, to have overturned an altar, smashed a sacred chalice, and even murdered a Melitian bishop in the course of his violent proceedings against the sectaries. As far as the last of these charges is concerned, Athanasius was able to vindicate himself. His secret service succeeded in tracing the alleged victim, who was hiding in a monastery in Upper Egypt and, when the wanted man escaped in time, he was later discovered in Tyre and identified by the bishop of that place. Complaints about acts of violence and illegal encroachments on the rights of others

6

accompanied the patriarch throughout his life. It is no longer possible to assess their credibility in every case. Athanasius rejected every complaint in the most violent terms. He knew how to hold his ground amid the press of intrigues and dishonest polemics and was a master at impressing the masses. His pamphlets reveal the intelligence and clarity of an outstanding personality, but at the same time they employ every possible means of defamation and constantly caricature his opponents in the most lurid colours. Blood was shed repeatedly in the Alexandrian struggles, and in his later years Athanasius came more than once near to committing high treason. But it was impossible to humble him, and he continued to believe in and assert his rights.

For a time it seemed as if Athanasius might win over the Emperor to his point of view. It is true that his enemies at court were at the helm of affairs and they had already been in touch with the Melitians in Egypt. But Athanasius refused to appear before their seat of judgment. When he finally had to present himself before a Council in Tyre he talked his way out by protesting uninterruptedly, and before sentence could be passed he had secretly escaped by sea. He turned up again in Constantinople, forcing himself on the Emperor and demanding an audience. In a letter the Emperor himself described how Athanasius had taken him completely by surprise. Even he clearly found it difficult to stand up face to face against this bishop's leonine fury. New discussions with his opponents were begun, but when they explained to the Emperor that Athanasius, whose predecessors had already played a great part in the Egyptian corn trade, was now about to cut off all supplies to the capital city, the Emperor's patience was exhausted. According to Athanasius's own account, Constantine became extremely angry and banished him to Trier without any further discussion. It was the first of five exiles which Athanasius underwent and which kept him away from his see for seventeen years altogether.

We cannot follow his story in any further detail, through all the ups and downs of political and ecclesiastical developments. Two circumstances above all made it possible for him to assert himself in the end. The first was the support that he found in the Latin world. The traditional good relationships between the sees of Alexandria and Rome were revived by his sojourn in the West. The whole of the West became consciously Athanasian. The difficult philosophical speculation which formed the background to the Arian controversy met with no understanding in the West, which took it for granted that there must be a close connection between the Father and the Son. There was in fact a widespread inclination to identify in practice the two persons of the Godhead—the greatest theological crime imaginable for a Greek theologian trained in the school of Origen!

In order that this Western sympathy might become effective a further purely political factor had to come into operation. Constantine had divided the Empire among his sons, and this had led to a loss of unity in the State's ecclesiastical politics. Each separate ruler now favoured the tendency prevailing in his own part of the Empire and strove to promote it to the best of his ability in the neighbouring zone as well. Thus the weaker son, Constantius, who ruled in the East, was twice forced by his brother to readmit Athanasius. The first time this happened was immediately after the death of Constantine in 337. Instead of going straight to Alexandria, Athanasius travelled for months on end through the provinces of Syria and Asia Minor in order to reinstate his party in the East and to strengthen its unity. When he was recalled after a further period of several years in exile in the West, in similar circumstances, he managed to exploit his victory even more intensely. The Emperor who had banished him was forced to invite Athanasius no less than three times before he would appear before him again in Antioch. He then travelled on by way of Jerusalem, where a synod was in session, entering his episcopal city in triumph.

When Constantius became sole ruler in 353 and was able to take action against Athanasius, the situation again seemed desperate. The issue was decided by a letter which Athanasius maintained was a forgery from which it appeared that he had been conspiring in the intervening period with a Western usurper. This time even the Western synods were compelled to drop Athanasius, and in spite of the furious opposition of the people of Alexandria an attempt was made to remove him by military force. Athanasius had, however, escaped in good time; he stayed in the city in successful concealment and organized the continuous resistance of his followers. Even when a successor had been appointed the riots went on and the struggle continued.

Looking at the tempestuous outward course of these events, one is tempted to interpret them as struggles for political power in the Church. This is precisely what Athanasius's opponents always maintained. They carefully avoided stressing the theological background of their opposition, and treated Athanasius simply as an obstinate trouble-maker, an intolerant, power-seeking hierarch but for whose wilfulness and violence the Church would have been living undisturbed and at peace.

This method of making purely political and criminal accusations was the surest way of reducing the theological opposition to silence when you had the power of the State on your side. In contrast to these not entirely honest tactics, Athanasius immediately lifted every controversy onto the theological plane. In a tone of supreme indignation he mercilessly declared that anyone who opposed him was a notorious heretic, a 'mad Arian', a blasphemer of Christ goaded by the meanest motives, and an enemy of the true Church. He admitted no doubts about the validity of his own position. The absolute self-confidence of his attack and defence gave his pamphlets the stormy atmosphere and booming echo which he needed for success. Athanasius was a very deliberate and determined propagandist for his cause. It must not, however, be inferred that the theological principles he claimed to be defending were mere pretexts and without any true significance for him. Athanasius believed in what he asserted. But he lacked all sense of the distance between the religious concerns which he represented and the ecclesiastical position that he wanted to hold. He did not really think of the Church as a sacramental institution but in terms of the sacred dogma which sustains it.

To all intents and purposes, however, belief, creed, and the Church—or rather, the ecclesiastical party which supported him —were all one to him. There was no such thing as a creed without followers, and their political exigencies were hallowed by the cause which was the object of the whole struggle. This is what gave rise to the unscrupulousness and self-righteousness and also the passion and reckless courage with which Athanasius fought his life's struggle, sacrificed his security and peace, his reputation and, when the need arose, even his friends. Thus he became the living symbol of orthodoxy and the unconquerable Church. He was the centre from which friend and foe alike had to take their bearings—a better and clearer one than the tangled formulas and decisions of Councils which accompanied the struggle round his personality.

In the main principles of his theology Athanasius remained constant. But the methods with which he carried on his struggle and the way in which he established and confirmed his theological position were subject to development. In his early period he had ingenuously appealed to the Emperor and striven to win his agreement. The personality of the holy Emperor-Liberator impelled him to certain indispensable considerations, though as we have seen his submissiveness to the Emperor had its limits in an emergency. His attitude to Constantius, who had none of his father's superior qualities, was quite different from the very outset. Athanasius was in almost continuous conflict with him, and more and more dropped all consideration for this 'patron of godlessness and Emperor of heresy' (*Hist. Ar.* 45, 4). The fact that the Arians had dared to trouble the Emperor at all with ecclesiastical affairs, that they submitted their synodal decisions to him for his confirmation and mobilized soldiers to enforce them, was now declared to be a 'scandalous crime' contrary to all canonic tradition: 'What has the Emperor to do with the Church?' (*Hist. Ar.* 52, 3). For the first time, the idea of 'Church freedom' was advocated, by Athanasius and his friends, against a Christian ruler. Even when one sees through the tactical motives that lay behind it, this is still a significant fact. From the standpoint of a Eusebian theology such a procedure would never have been possible.

Athanasius also developed in his method of dogmatic controversy. In the early years he hardly made any use of the Nicene Creed. The proofs of the absolute deity of Christ were purely objective and Biblical, and anyone who curtailed them was, as we have seen, at once denounced as an 'Arian', even after Arius himself had long since disappeared from the scene and died or, as Athanasius avers, 'split into pieces in the public lavatory' (*De Morte Ar.* 3, 3). He only gradually came to see the possibilities which the concept of Homoousios ('of one substance') used in the Nicene Creed contained for his own theological position, whereas it could never be accepted by his Arian and Eusebian opponents. He proceeded regularly to refer to this sacred Council and its Creed as the one sure shield of orthodoxy. He made recognition of its authority the indispensable condition for genuine pacification. Athanasius thus created the conception of the first 'ecumenical' synod. The Nicene, or later the expanded Niceno-Constantinopolitan Creed, has been regarded ever since as the sole or at least the only permanently authoritative and valid Creed of the Christian Faith. Its very exclusiveness and rigidity provided a welcome opportunity for deriding as transparently godless manœuvres the new formulas which were constantly being used by the opponents of Athanasius in their efforts to accommodate themselves to changing circumstances in ecclesiastical politics. According to Athanasius, the truth has long since been discovered and a genuinely serious theology can consist only in the interpretation of what the Church has already established once and for all.

In his own thinking, however, Athanasius remained thoroughly flexible. His obstinacy was not intended to promote the formulas as such, but the cause of his party and of the one unchanging truth concealed in the Nicene symbol. Towards the end of his life he gave an impressive proof of this. At bottom he was interested in only one thing: the complete and absolute divinity and unity with God of the Logos Christ who became man. Because of this he had for a long time left in peace those friends who did not make a clear distinction of any kind between the two divine persons. At first he ignored as a dubious or unnecessary speculation the idea of three interrelated Hypostases within the one divine Being. But theology could not remain static, and once again it was developments in the world of ecclesiastical politics that opened Athanasius's eyes and took him a further step forward.

In the last years of his rule Constantius came nearer and nearer to a radically Arian position, and the policy of 'unification' which he was following no longer affected only Athanasius and the strict upholders of the Nicene Creed. Many members of the former party of the centre and the younger generation of theologians felt no less affronted and attempted to get in touch with like-minded theologians of the 'right' wing in order to obtain their support in the fight against the unscrupulously opportunistic policy of the ruling Churchmen. They might have been able to accept the Nicene Creed but they were afraid of the idea of the complete identity of the divine persons which it seemed to encourage. Thus Athanasius decided to take a firm stand against this interpretation and to acknowledge the feasibility of the three Hypostases, provided that the inseparable unity of the one divine Being was clearly preserved. The decisive offer of peace was made in the year 362 at a synod in Alexandria, the background of which was the change in the Church's situation under the new pagan Emperor Julian. Julian had allowed all the exiles to return and appeared determined to leave the Church entirely to itself and its own bickerings. The policy of coercion pursued hitherto had collapsed, and the way was open for a regrouping and a fresh agreement among the parties. The work of reconciliation was not achieved so quickly as Athanasius had probably hoped; but a beginning was made and the final assembly of the right-wing group which came about years later originated in the policy initiated in the year 362.

To begin with, it was a matter of surviving a new wave of repression on the part of the State. In his attempt to revive the old pagan worship Julian had met the universal resistance of the Church, and Athanasius was the last man to make any sort of concessions to the romantic on the imperial throne. He was soon compelled to vacate his see again. But this kind of thing had apparently ceased to make much impression on him. It is said that he comforted the broken-hearted crowd that pressed around him as he said farewell, with the words that became famous: 'Do not be led astray, brethren; it is but a little cloud and it will quickly pass' (Ruf. *H.E.* I, 34: *Nolite, o filii, conturbari, quia nubicula est et cito pertransibit*). He proved to be right. Once again Athanasius was forced into exile under Julian's 'Arian' successor. Then peace gradually descended on his life. The government had probably reached the conclusion that the simplest thing would be to leave Athanasius in peace in Egypt, in spite of his refractoriness, rather than to inflame the people, who were devoted to him, by repeated intervention. When he died in the year 373 victory had not yet been achieved throughout the Empire, but a few years later the new Emperor Theodosius from the West brought the whole development to a close by declaring that all his subjects were to regard the Nicene Creed as a binding authority. What the strongest political and theological personality in the Church of the fourth century had striven for had become established.

Even to his own contemporaries Athanasius seemed an almost mythical figure; even pagans credited him with supernatural knowledge. In later ages he was regarded as the incomparable 'pillar of the Church', through whom God had protected and preserved the true Faith in a most difficult period (Greg. Naz. *Or.* 21, 26). 'If you find something of the writings of St. Athanasius,' an abbot of the sixth century wrote, 'and you have no paper handy, write it on your clothes' (Joh. Mosch. *Prat. Spir.* 40). His works—the authentic as well as the innumerable unauthentic ones which were put out under the protection of his name—enjoyed a circulation in accordance with his high reputation. From a historical point of view, however, his importance lies not so much in his writings themselves as in the things he defended and sustained by his actions in a life full of tension and disturbance. In an unusually critical moment in the Church's history, when all the old ideas and organizations were being transformed and rebuilt in the new Church of Constantine, he maintained the essential character and spiritual independence of Christianity in his struggles with the emperors and all the authoritative representatives of the theological world. As a result of his labours, belief in Christ remained, in the strictest sense, belief in God and was kept distinct from all pagan, philosophical, and idealistic theories. But for him, as Harnack has said (*Lehrbuch d. Dogmengeschichte* II [1909⁴], 224), the Church would probably have fallen completely into the hands of the philosophers (of the Eusebian type); its creed would have run wild or become an imperial regulation governing the worship of the 'radiant Godhead'. Athanasius saved the Church from becoming entangled in the idea of cultural progress and from the snares of political power. Through him it again became an institute of salvation, that is, a Church in the strict sense of the word, with the preaching of Christ as its essential purpose. It is no accident that the Church came to be regarded as an autonomous body in the legal sense, the independence of which must be preserved in all circumstances.

We have already pointed out that this also involved a new departure within the Church itself. Athanasius was the first Greek Father who did not regard himself as a 'Christian philosopher' but who, even as a theologian, remained the bishop. As such he sought to bridge the gap between theology and the mass of Church members and their devotion. Unlike Clement and Origen, he did not regard spiritual 'perfection' as the affair of a select circle of highly educated Gnostics and intellectuals. He addressed himself to the organized celibates within the Church, he ventured to preach in Coptic, and if he was forced on the one hand to carry the watchwords of the theological conflict to the masses he took their crude ideas of holiness and their belief in miracles as his point of departure. He succeeded in getting in touch with the religious revival movement which erupted from the very depths of the Egyptian people, and so he managed to steer it into the paths of the development and devotion of the Universal Church. That was certainly not the least of his historical services. Athanasius discovered monasticism and gave it the form in which from now on it permeated the Greek Church in its multifarious developments and ramifications and also determined the clerical way of life and the fundamental religious conceptions of the theologians.

The beginnings of Egyptian monasticism are older than Athanasius; they go back to the second half of the third century. The monastic movement was the result of the wholesale conversion of the flat lands, which had hardly been touched by Greek civilization, and of their primitive fellaheen population. These people seized on the old ascetic commandments of the Church with a new enthusiasm and tried to carry them out unconditionally in the deep solitude of the desert rather than inside the local churches. In this respect 'Father' Anthony was only one of many similar contemporary figures. It was Athanasius, who knew him personally, who made him the 'inventor' and prototype of eremitic monasticism. The book in which he described his life introduced the Church to a new phenomenon and stimulated universal imitation and emulation. Even in the story of the conversion of Augustine the *Vita Antonii* plays a part, and innumerable Greek lives of the saints were planned on the pattern which it had established. In his account of Anthony's life Athanasius kept to the facts, but he described monasticism in the way in which he wanted to see and promote it. The little book was not written without apologetic and propagandistic intentions. Without detriment to his simple and original nature, Anthony was presented as the incarnation of the philosophical virtues which are truly to be found only in Christians and can be acquired only through the power and grace of Christ. At the same time he attacked the pagan sages and Arian heretics and showed a profound and sincere regard for all the representatives of the spiritual estate. The saint sets the pattern for the Church by experiencing and effecting the greatest things in his ascetic zeal: he receives illuminations and becomes the instrument of supernatural powers. The ascetic ideal was presented to educated and uneducated alike as a new and alluring way of life, and yet it remained clearly established on Christ and the orthodox teaching of the Church. In this sense Athanasius strove to combine monasticism with Nicene orthodoxy and blended them in the depth of popular feeling and the consciousness of the Church.

The theologians who succeeded Athanasius continued to be Origenists, philosophers, and Greeks. But they did not dissolve the solid unity into which he had fused the claims of dogma, asceticism, and the Church. In the fourth century that unity became universally predominant. Athanasius himself had been above all a dogmatist and a hierarch and as such an ecclesiastical politician. But with him and his generation a new era began in the life of the Greek Church in the inner realm of theology and spiritual life as well.

CHAPTER VII

BASIL THE GREAT

ABOUT the time that Athanasius was made a bishop, possibly ten years before the death of Eusebius of Caesarea, Basil was born. The Church in which Basil grew up was recognized and assisted by the State, and all the political, social, and intellectual currents of the 'world' were coming to be accepted in it. The Church had become an outstanding factor in public life. Its bishops often found themselves in glittering positions and enjoyed public esteem and wealth and extensive spheres of influence. There was a strong tendency to a more cultural and opportunistic type of Christianity, though this was sadly or mockingly criticized by keen-sighted observers both inside and outside the Church. The question as to the religious foundations of the Church which had been raised by the Arian controversy had still not been decided. Many Churchmen were trying to avoid making a decision, by abandoning themselves to general activities with a devotional trimming. On the other hand, the message of Christ was threatening to become the subject of all kinds of theological conflict. The imperial government was endeavouring to limit the boundless tension and controversy and to hold the Church together by occasional decrees, synodal resolutions, and coercive measures. No one's conscience was quite reconciled to all this, but most of the bishops sought somehow to come to terms with the elastic formulas which were being offered or silently to slip out of the predicament. They made a habit of ignoring protests and more or less openly let theology go to the devil. In a period of outwardly brilliant material and cultural progress the Church was threatened with decline and the loss of its conscience. In the process of attempting to master the situation the possibility of responsible action in the future was being slowly but surely blocked.

This is the background against which the personality and work of Basil 'the Great' have to be seen. Basil was essentially an ascetic and a theologian. As such he opened up a path for his endangered contemporaries; but he was in strong and conscious opposition to the great mass of his episcopal colleagues. As a 'young Nicaean', Basil was a follower of the aged Athanasius; he continued his life's struggle in another geographical sphere and in a different theological spirit. But although he personally was spared from exile and serious injury, he found it much more difficult to assert himself, since Cappadocia was nothing like so self-contained an ecclesiastical province as Egypt. Basil had also to contend with greater spiritual problems because he was a far more sensitive nature and a more richly endowed character who felt the ambiguities of the enervating struggle more deeply and suffered more keenly than the inflexible old Patriarch of Alexandria.

As a man and a theologian Basil was not rooted in the clerical world, and his character was not moulded to begin with by the struggles of ecclesiastical politics. Pride and independence were native to him from the very outset. As a Christian he deliberately repressed these qualities, but his self-assurance was based on the memories of a great family and an ancient countryside which was just exposing itself to the Christian life on the broadest front.

According to an often quoted remark of Mommsen's, the formerly Hittite and then Persian province of Cappadocia was 'hardly more Greek at the beginning of the imperial age than Brandenburg and Pomerania were French under Frederick the Great' (*Röm. Gesch.* V, ch. 8). Christianity had been disseminated here by Gregory Thaumaturgus, the disciple of Origen, and may in turn have spread the influence of Hellenism. Both forces, Hellenism and Christianity, were a jointly accepted tradition in Basil's family. His grandparents were Christians and had had to escape for a time during the last persecution under Maximinus. An uncle, then two brothers, were, like Basil himself, made bishops, and his sister Macrina dedicated herself entirely to the ascetic life. Higher education in the Hellenist spirit was as much taken for granted in this family as Christian, that is, Nicene-Christian, education. His father did not want Basil to receive a 'one-eyed' education (Greg. Naz. Or. 43, 12) but to enjoy a full classical and philosophical training. In view of the princely wealth of the family, derived from estates which were spread over three provinces, there were no financial obstacles.

Basil began his studies in Cappadocian Caesarea when he was about fifteen years old, and he continued them in Constantinople. He spent the decisive terms in Athens from 351 onwards. Gregory of Nazianzus, with whom he entered upon a lifelong friendship at this period, later recorded how he had saved his friend from the exploitation to which freshmen were usually subjected, and he asserted that in their ardent passion for study they had spent their whole time in the lecture room or in church.

We may take into account, besides the desire for sanctification which Gregory emphasizes, his social position and an early sense of intellectual superiority. At any rate in these years Basil acquired a comprehensive education. His writings show that he retained a lifelong intimacy with Plato, Homer, and the historians and rhetors, and they certainly influenced his style. He felt no embarrassment in his contacts with pagans. He knew the famous orator Libanius personally, and had some correspondence with him. Basil never became an enthusiast for culture like Gregory, however, and as a monk and bishop he later looked back somewhat critically on the 'idle rapture' of the period in Athens (Greg. Naz. Or. 43, 11). Basil did not ignore the moral dangers of classical literature, but the advice that he gave to his nephew on what books he should study shows that he was not prepared on that account to renounce the treasures of classical learning. The important thing was to choose one's reading with care. He denied that the pagan writers had anything more than a purely propaedeutic significance (that is, serving as an introduction to higher study), but their usefulness was not limited to the merely formal and aesthetic aspects; they were welcome aids in the moral education of the Christian too.

It seems that Basil himself wavered between the possibilities of the career of a rhetor and his Christian ideals. He returned home 'a ship heavily laden with culture' (Greg. Naz. *Or.* 43, 21). He was sought after on every side, and every public career stood open to him. But he broke resolutely away. He did not want to serve the 'world', and he became baptized in order to begin a purely ascetic life according to the Lord's commandment. It is not quite clear how he came to make this decision. The family tradition, his sister's zealous persuasion, the impression made on him by a journey through the hermitages of Egypt, all these things probably played a part. Basil had also probably received a decisive stimulus from an earlier ascetic movement in his homeland, and especially from a man whom he greatly admired at the time and came to despise later on: Eustathius of Sebaste, in Lesser Armenia. This pioneer of the monastic ideal had also attracted many followers in Cappadocia, so that he was regarded with suspicion by some of the bishops who were but little inclined to intense asceticism. Basil, however, became his disciple. Much of what he taught about the monastic life and the art of spiritual guidance probably derived from Eustathius. The two men separated later on for dogmatic reasons. Eustathius opposed the Nicene Creed and was thereupon decried as an 'Arian'; and at this juncture the Creed was more important for Basil than the old friendship and fellowship in the service of ascetic ideals. He did not want a Christianity that ignored dogma.

To be understood, Basil must nevertheless be studied primarily as a monk. He was an ascetic, body and soul; strict asceticism was the element in which he lived and moved and had his spiritual being. He was an ascetic to the extent to which it is possible to be one without conflicting with the Church and its Christian doctrine. He respected these limits throughout his life, however, and in Cappadocia this was not unimportant. Basil never turned the monastic life against the Church, never believed it was impossible for married Christians to be saved, as the followers of Eustathius came to do. For him even the strictest asceticism was not dualistically motivated in a Marcionite or Manichaean sense. Basil remained in this a 'Greek'. Doubtless, his thinking was based on the antithesis between flesh and spirit, earth and heaven, time and eternity, and the eschatological point of view always played a very vital part in his theological thinking; but the physical and temporal world was, in his view, not evil in itself, but merely a constant incitement to evil. Only that life is completely meaningful that is based on the spirit, on God and his blessed eternity. But by striving after this goal and subjecting himself to hard training and self-discipline the monk does not destroy his true human self. On the contrary, his true self is liberated, furnished with wings, and raised up beyond the constricting barriers, that it may give itself wholly to God, see God, and become one with God.

This conception derives from Neoplatonic metaphysics and the ideas of Basil's beloved master, Origen. But Basil lays greater emphasis than all his predecessors, with the possible exception of Clement, on the point that the real power of this liberated life is not merely knowledge but love, love not only in the 'theological' sense of love for God but also love for one's neighbour. For Basil the monastic life is therefore fundamentally a life in community where all can serve one another and each can be helped and developed by the other, thus becoming the true life in which all human potentialities are sublimated, the Christian life par excellence.

What happened in fact is that Basil retired to the estates which his family owned on the river Iris and where his mother and sister had already been living for a long time in pious seclusion. He gathered together like-minded companions who submitted to his leadership and established further monasteries to which he offered spiritual instruction and advice. The discipline was strict, obedience absolute, humility in all things the spiritual goal. In addition to spiritual contemplation the monks did simple manual labour. A return to the world was impossible. But the spirit and atmosphere of these communities were not intended to be ridden with rules and regulations: the brethren lived in freedom of the spirit. Prayer is the sustaining power of monastic life; the fixed hours of praise and prayer give it a rhythmic pattern. The greatest importance was attached to the interchange of the brothers. In their meetings they were able to air their various desires, problems, and questions quite freely. They were able to have their own spiritual counsellors and later on themselves became the spiritual counsellors of other monks. The regular practice of monastic confession derives above all from Basil. This life did not exclude delight in intellectual work and theological knowledge. For most of the brothers, however, the central activity was the study of the Bible and especially of the writings of Paul and the Synoptic Gospels. It was, however, at this time that Basil compiled the *Anthology* from Origen's writings in co-operation with his friend Gregory.

As a monk Basil was wholly himself. The powers with which he was able to overcome the ever-present temptations, to know God's truth and enjoy every 'divine beauty', increased in the beloved peace and quiet of the cloister. The famous letter (*Ep. 14, ad Greg.*) in which he tried to entice Gregory, who was still living at a distance, to join him is a surprising document in this respect. The description of his hermitage, which offers him a splendid view high up in the valley near a waterfall, and has given him peace at last in the midst of the unsullied freshness of nature, is the first deeply-felt description of a landscape known to the Western world—an ancient idyll which has something of a foreboding mystery that places it outside all traditional categories.

Anyone who is able to enjoy solitude to that extent cannot expect it to last for ever. Basil was far too much a man of action, or at least of actively moral responsibility, to be able to stay

7

undisturbed for ever in this beloved way of life. Theological cares and obligations drew him irresistibly back into the public life of the Church. At this period the Emperor's anti-Nicene policy had just reached its most relentless stage. In the year 360 Basil accompanied Eustathius to Constantinople for negotiations on dogmatic matters. The Nicene party was not quite so weak as it seemed, but it lacked the courage to declare itself openly. Two years later Basil received the penitent confession of his own bishop, who had betrayed the Nicene Creed but called Basil to his deathbed.

The new Bishop Eusebius of Caesarea (in Cappadocia, not Palestine, where the famous Eusebius had been bishop) succeeded in drawing Basil into the full-time service of the Church. In the year 364 he was ordained presbyter. The proud country nobleman was probably not a comfortable subordinate; perhaps his ascetic zeal also made him distrusted. Tensions soon arose between the presbyter and his bishop, with the result that Basil, who had no desire for quarrels within the Church, suddenly decided to return to his hermitage.

This interruption did not, however, last for long. Eusebius himself sought for a reconciliation, and Basil did not hesitate to come to terms with him. The Church needed his work. He now rapidly grew into the role of a coadjutor of his bishop, and as such it was his task to administer a large diocese. He did not evade the irritating details and guerilla warfare of everyday life in the Church. As usual, everywhere there was a lack of really useful clergy, conscientious preachers, and selfless rulers. Out of sheer laziness the Church had often appointed quite unsuitable men to positions of responsibility. Offices had been bought and cases of bribery had occurred; there were married clergy who refused to give up their wives, and besides all the dogmatic conflicts there were the usual party bickerings, slander, and gossip. Basil took strong action where it was a question of reinforcing hitherto neglected ecclesiastical regulations. But he always tried to give intelligible reasons for his measures. He discussed them with his bishops, and whenever complaints were made he was always willing to take the blame himself. A generous nature, with an innate dignity, he had no difficulty in achieving a true balance between the demands his office made on him and the personal humility he had to maintain as a Christian and a monk. Basil became the first great representative of the monastic ideal of the priest and bishop, to whom the age that followed referred back again and again.

He soon became popular with the people of Caesarea. He created, no doubt very largely from his own resources, a whole complex of charitable welfare institutions. There arose a whole 'new city' (Greg. Naz. Or. 43, 63) of neighbourly love and social care grouped around the church and monastery, consisting of hostels, almshouses, and hospitals for infectious diseases, and the bishop himself took up residence there. The foundation was imitated and much admired, and also criticized. It was regarded as a threat to the independence of the State administration, an objection which Basil himself refused to accept. The early Christian activity in works of love was acquiring new 'medieval' dimensions in the imperial Church; the spirit that inspired these works of charity was more monastic than political and hierarchic. It was not intended that the laity should sink back into passivity. Basil's sermons were full of practical exhortations and examples, stimulating to acts of Christian love and the practice of virtue. Especially during the great famine of the year 368 he proved his mettle in impressive sermons against the profiteers and the indifferent rich. He himself organized free meals for the people which were also available to immigrant foreigners, pagans, and even the infidel children of Israel.

It would be wrong, however, to judge Basil primarily as an ecclesiastical man of action and an administrator. In the midst of his affairs and above all in his preaching he was always at the same time the pastor and the theologian. Basil is regarded as the initiator of the formal sermon in Greek. He deliberately moulded the religious address according to the rules of rhetoric, thus establishing a precedent. This carefully cultivated oratorical splendour, with its artificial and flowery display, is something quite strange to us today in religious diction; what is far more fascinating in Basil is the vigorous down-to-earthness, the precision and simplicity of his basic ideas, which nevertheless distinguish his sermons. Nearly all of them are based on Biblical texts. The moral sermon predominates, but even the theological sermons are not purely theoretical and 'dogmatic' in the bad sense of the word. They reflect the actual dogmatic conflicts of the contemporary Church in which Basil had to take a stand and in which he soon gained a position of authority.

In the year 370 he was made Archbishop of Caesarea, and from that time on the whole responsibility and worry of the confused situation in the Church rested above all on him. At this juncture there was no such thing as a united Nicene front. Basil himself used the simile of two fighting fleets which have been whirled together by the tempest so that it is impossible to distinguish friend from foe. It was only through his influence that Cappadocia slowly became something like a bulwark of the orthodox Church, though the conflict still raged all around it. The government's ecclesiastical policy was still heading in another direction and everywhere put obstacles in the way of Basil whose instructions were to co-operate with the political authorities. The division of the province of Cappadocia, which was intended to lessen the ecclesiastical influence of Caesarea, must also be mentioned here. Basil refused to be intimidated. He travelled in person from place to place, trying to tie the threads more closely together, establishing new dioceses, and conducting an indefatigable correspondence in all directions. The tension reached its climax when the Emperor Valens made a personal visit to Caesarea. It was expected that Basil would either surrender or go into exile. He did neither. It seems that the calm determination with which he stood up to the autocrat persuaded the Emperor to move cautiously and avoid a conflict. Nicene orthodoxy was gaining ground all the time in Cappadocia.

The successes which Basil achieved are to be reckoned the

more highly inasmuch as to begin with his position was anything but secure. Unlike Athanasius, he did not possess a band
of blindly devoted followers ready to go with him through
thick and thin. Perhaps he would not have wanted that kind of
support. His successes were primarily the fruit of the genuine
ecclesiastical and theological work which he carried out with
his friends, building on the foundation of the earlier Nicene-
Origenistic tradition of the country. Basil realized that the conflict with the Arians was due to an elemental conflict of belief.
Christ cannot be a creature if he is to make available the salvation of the Creator. He was really God's Son before all time
and God by nature, who came down to our poor humanity to
redeem lost mankind from the power of death and the devil
and to restore the freedom on which the new Christian life,
transfigured by grace, is based. Basil was a fully convinced
Trinitarian theologian and saw in the doctrine of the Trinity the
very essence of the Christian religion. He began therefore with
a systematic clarification of the relationships which exist within
the Godhead. Going beyond Athanasius, he underlined the
Trinity of the 'Hypostases', the segregating peculiarities of
which do not destroy the unity and completeness of the divine
Life. He also meditated on their mutual relationship. Such reflections never became an end in themselves; they were not
driven to death. There must always be a meaning which can at
least be conjectured behind dogmatic statements, and above all
they must be based on the Scriptures. In spite of the pressure
of his friends and enemies, Basil refused to make more precise
assertions about the person of the Holy Spirit which would
have been mere words. It is true that for him, as for Origen,
the Holy Spirit unquestionably has its place alongside the
Father and the Son. In the scale of being, that there can be
nothing between the uncreated Godhead and the creature is a
foregone conclusion, to which he repeatedly drew attention.
Nevertheless he avoided as far as possible roundly describing
the Spirit as 'God', and he was quite silent about the Spirit's
peculiar position within the Trinity. On the contrary, he

'confesses without fear' that the best thing and also the least 'dangerous' is frankly to admit one's ignorance (*Contra Sab. et Ar.* 24, 6).

We come across such admonitions in Basil again and again. There is not the least naïveté in this deliberate confinement to the 'simplicity of sound belief'. Basil realizes that the mania for controversy has brought the Church to the edge of the abyss and dissolution. He wants to avoid adding any new fuel to the fire of boundless dispute; he wants rather to set bounds to all the scholastic logic-chopping and lead the faithful to spiritual composure and adoring praise of the mystery of God. This was in his view the real purpose of all theology. Where the Bible is silent, theologians should be silent too and not upset people with their splitting of hairs. Man knows God by keeping his commandments, by knowing the Good Shepherd who gave his life for the sheep, and 'not by asking questions about supra-mundane things, and not by pondering over the things one cannot see' (*Hom. in Mam. Mart.* 4). These are unmistakably monastic motifs, pointed by the bitter experiences of a long ecclesiastical struggle. Only Basil had no wish to escape alto-gether from theology and end up with a mere *praxis pietatis.* He wanted to establish the foundations for the fruitful kind of theology which would draw together all true and serious theologians.

To this extent his reserve on matters of dogma also had a significance for church politics. This is especially clear in relation to the doctrine of the Spirit. Basil made the greatest efforts to win over the so-called Pneumatomachians, who appealed to Nicaea and refused to accept the divinity of the Holy Spirit, which had not been expressly formulated there. He also tried to enter into discussion with representatives of the so-called Centre Party and with many doctrinal individualists. His efforts were not without success, but it is not surprising that the liberality of an attitude with both theological and ecclesi-astical significance did not make things any easier for a Church-man who had to maintain his position in the midst of party warfare. Basil's lack of principle, or his spiritual pride, was commented on in all kinds of quarters, though he attempted to refute the criticism again and again by always offering to enter conversations and discussions. A highly important factor was that Athanasius gave Basil his utmost support. In spite of certain theological differences, he had discerned the outstanding significance of this comrade in arms and acknowledged it throughout his life.

Basil realized from the outset that the Church's dogmatic problems could not be solved on a particularistic basis. It is true that it would have been comparatively easy for him to keep to his own Cappadocian circle, where his authority was unquestioned anyway. But he would have regarded that as a betrayal of the common cause of all Christians. Basil required an 'ecumenical' outlook of all bishops. Contrary to appearances, there is a unity, a single voice of the true believers throughout the world. The important thing is to be seriously concerned about 'the brotherhood which exists everywhere' (Ep. 133 ad Petr. Alex.), which puts its members in touch with one another and thereby makes the unity visible and effective. This was the end served by Basil's gigantic and ever-increasing correspondence. 'Ask the Pisidians, Lycaonians, and Isaurians, the inhabitants of both parts of Phrygia, the Armenians, in so far as they are your neighbours, the Macedonians, Greeks, Illyrians, Gauls, Spaniards, the whole of Italy, the Sicilians, Africans, the sound centre part of Egypt and what is left of [orthodox] Syria, who all send letters to me and also receive replies from me': this is what Basil once wrote to Pontus (Ep. 204, 7 ad Neocaes.).

Apart from the old bulwarks of orthodoxy, Rome and Alexandria, a new centre arose in which, as was soon to appear, an independent line was to be followed. All Basil's endeavours were based on the assumption that the important thing was to apply the weight of the Nicene West to a corresponding reformation of the Eastern Church, though preserving the latter's character and theological comprehensiveness as far as possible. He overcame the innate pride of the Greek and turned to his

Western colleagues for help, imploring their 'sympathy'. He turned above all to the most important of them, Bishop Damasus of Rome.

There were special difficulties to be overcome in Antioch, and it was here that Basil hoped the Pope would intervene in the first instance. The great majority of the orthodox Antiochenes acknowledged Bishop Meletius as their bishop. After some initial doubts he had come out clearly on the side of the Nicene Creed. Unfortunately, however, a small band of irreconcilable old campaigners had championed a stricter adherent of the Nicene Creed. The opposition between old and young Nicaeans which Athanasius had overcome had broken out in the capital of Syrian Christianity again. It became more intense and threatened to wreck the whole work of unification. Basil at once supported Meletius. He knew very well that the West, which found it almost impossible to grasp the finer distinctions which caused these dogmatic conflicts, inclined to the opposition party and would have preferred to speak quite plainly of the one divine Hypostasis. But he took the view that now that theological peace between the two orthodox camps had been declared it was possible to reckon on Rome's understanding and to win Damasus's support for the one feasible method of reaching a settlement. He was mistaken. Damasus, who has been called the 'first Pope' and who almost had the outward airs of a prince, was only moderately interested in theological problems; to him church unification meant, in a sentence, favouring partisans of Rome and securing subjection to Papal authority. The negotiations were therefore inconclusive, to begin with. Basil gave vent to his feeling about this way of caring for the churches in these bitter words: 'I am reminded of the words of Diomedes (Il. IX, 698 f.): It is futile to implore, for the man is presumptuous' (Ep. 215 ad Euseb. Sam.). In other respects too Basil was driven to the brink of bitterness and contempt in his struggle with the hydra of the party spirit. But he did not slacken his efforts, and gradually he gained ground.

Basil himself was not to attain the goal of his endeavours. He wore himself out before his time. Ill and suffering from a liver complaint, like so many ascetics, he died at the age of about fifty in the year 379. Two years later there took place in Constantinople, under the chairmanship of Meletius, the so-called second Ecumenical Council, which the Emperor Theodosius the Great used in order to reorganize the Eastern Church on the lines laid down by the Nicene Creed. Athanasius and Basil had already laid the ecclesiastical and theological foundations. Theodosius, the Westerner, had also, in the beginning, based his policy on the Rome-Alexandria 'axis' but quickly changed his mind. As Basil had wished, he now opened the gates of the revived Imperial Church to everyone who accepted the Nicene Creed, and he ignored the protests of the steadfast old Nicaeans of East and West. But this was a settlement brought about for purely practical reasons. At the critical moment ecclesiastical politics proved far stronger than theology. If Basil had still been alive things would probably have taken a different and happier course. The age of the epigoni was dawning.

Basil's true greatness becomes apparent only when he is studied in the context of the conflicts of his age and his role is properly understood. As an ecclesiastical politician Basil did not display the rocklike strength of Athanasius; as a theologian he did not possess the harmony and universality of his younger brother, Gregory of Nyssa; as a monk he did not possess the subtle refinement of some of the later mystics. But these things must not be interpreted as signs of natural incapacity or a weakness in his character. On the contrary, it was his very devotion to the needs of the hour, the necessity of adapting himself to the difficulties of his situation, which compelled him constantly to vary his tactics and made it impossible for him to develop his rich talents in peace or follow the bent of his spirit as he wished. He found his work as an ecclesiastical politician so difficult because he was not only wiser and more far-seeing but also more profound and more honest than most of his colleagues.

It is thanks to him in the first place that the State Church of the Nicenes, which had been built so quickly, not only celebrated easy victories but retained a real theological life and intellectual freedom. Whereas others never progressed beyond the theology of their school, never saw beyond their party interests and purely material considerations, Basil had always kept in view the whole life of the Church. He suffered from the narrow-mindedness and lack of spiritual insight of his fellow-bishops far more than those who were too other-worldly, too sensitive, or too complacent to enter the fray themselves. And Basil discerned, beyond the worries and problems of the moment, profound changes which had to be accepted. He realized it was impossible to put the clock back.

From the historical point of view this is perhaps the most interesting aspect of his character. Basil sensed the gulf that had arisen between the intentions and desires of the present and the original spirit of Christianity. Again and again he contrasts the sins of the present with the Church as once it had been. The longing for an ideal original Christianity corresponded in his theology to the longing for eternal perfection. That is why Basil became a monk. The monastic community revived for him, within a strictly limited sphere, the life of the early Church, and his intention was that the monastic life should influence the whole Church in this direction. The idea was that in monastic life the spiritual gifts, the primal love, the devoted intensity of mutual relationships, should flourish once again. This was the purpose behind the so-called 'Rule' which he formulated. Monastic asceticism was regarded as the way to the radicalism and sanctity of the early Church. And Basil also hoped that this would lead to a revival of theology. The endless dogmatic arguments and disputes were no longer concerned, in his view, with the substance and basic problems of the Christian Faith. What was needed was an attempt to return to the beginnings again, to the eternal validities, to overcome the dissension and the errors of the heretics from within. The emphatic Biblicism to which Basil withdrew again and again was rooted in this conviction. It was a confession of faith in the old ecclesiastical tradition.

Both factors, the Bible and tradition, had already played an important part in the Church in the second century. They were closely related in Origen. But whereas he saw the task as one of advancing ever further away from tradition, Basil turned back rather to Irenaeus. Basil stood for confinement rather than further expansion. It was only the heretics' mania for innovation that made it necessary to evolve more and more complicated formulas. In their vain jealousy the professional theologians set their 'traps' not for the sake of truth but for the mere sake of argument (*De Spir. S.* 1). 'We refuse to accept a new faith, prescribed to us by others; but we are not bold enough to transmit the products of our own thinking and to turn the word of religion into human words. As we have been taught by the holy Fathers so we proclaim it to those who inquire of us' (*Ep. 140, 2 ad Eccl. Ant.*). Dogma and tradition again assume a decidedly defensive purpose, as a shield and safeguard. Indefatigably Basil advises all Christians to keep to the Nicene Creed and not be lured away from it by any subtle, captious questions.

Karl Holl speaks in this connection of a perceptible 'aging of Hellenism'. The expression does not seem quite appropriate. It was not Hellenism that had grown old and tired, at least not in the person of Basil the Great, but the burden of the ecclesiastical situation and the advances in theology had begun to weigh heavily on the freedom of research and were forcing theologians to consolidate and contain their energies rather than make fresh advances. What now seemed pre-eminently necessary was the stabilizing and stability of dogma, a clear commitment to the Bible and authoritative traditions. It is clear that this old necessity meant something different in the fourth century from what it did in the age of Justin or Clement, of Origen or even Eusebius of Caesarea. To that extent there is a sense in which it is true to say that the Greek Church had aged, because its theological traditions had aged and one does feel that an epoch in the Church's history was coming to an end. Basil felt the gravity of the situation, but amidst the almost desperate dangers of the time he thought above all of the need to concentrate all available forces against the heretics and to restore peace in the Church, that it might lead a truly spiritual life again. He was not concerned with the fate of theology in the future because he was truly absorbed in its present life and felt a strong sense of responsibility to give it all he could of his own spiritual vitality.

In the year 368 Basil wrote an obituary notice on Bishop Musonius of Neo-Caesarea which paints in noble diction and with rhetorical verve the picture of a leading bishop whom he came nearest to resembling himself. 'Is there', he asks (*Ep. 28, 1 ad Eccl. Neocaes.*), 'in the life of this man any feature which ought to be forgotten or silently concealed? I cannot mention everything at once and yet I am afraid of not doing justice to the truth by rendering a piecemeal account. A man has gone from us who surpassed all his contemporaries in human capacity; he was the support of his homeland, the adornment of his churches, a pillar and bulwark of the truth, a firm support of the Christian Faith, a loyal helper of his friends, an unconquerable might of resistance to his enemies, a keeper of the statutes of the Fathers, and an enemy of all innovation. He embodied in his own person the ancient pattern of the Church; he moulded the life of the Church set under him according to the original holy prototype. Those who were privileged to live with him might think they had lived with the men who illuminated the world like stars two hundred and more years ago.'

CHAPTER VIII

GREGORY OF NAZIANZUS

I<small>T</small> is traditional to combine in the trinity of the 'great Cappadocians' Basil and his slightly older friend Gregory of Nazianzus and his younger brother Gregory of Nyssa. But Basil was
the outstanding figure, the leader and guide of his friends and
collaborators. Gregory of Nazianzus became his follower and
sought his help; he also regarded him as his teacher theologically. With deep intensity, he took up the new ascetic piety
for which Basil enlisted supporters, and was equally anxious
to see it influential in the Church. Gregory was not, however,
a dominating personality and was constantly being thwarted
by the hard and common realities which he ignored in his
thinking. He was a rhetorician, a man of letters and something
of a poet, a soft lyrical nature who was always dependent on
the company and response of other people, one of those personalities that cannot live without sympathy and admiration.
This was what impelled him into the public life of the Church,
which constituted for him, by his upbringing and conviction,
the whole of his world. But the stormy times did not allow him
to develop his talents in peace and constantly involved him, a
man who was strong only in his words, in tasks to which he
was not equal and which he had to give up. Disappointment
and defeat, retreat and flight from the obligations he had undertaken, were always the end; to make up for all his troubles and
pains he sings the praises of the solitary life, of the life of 'philosophical' monastic contemplation, of richness and silence in
God, with all the greater enthusiasm. The fact that Gregory's
nervous, oratorical nature made it impossible for him ever to
be really silent made the situation all the more painful; all his

personal bitterness, vanity, and bad temper found expression in
a never-ending run of skilfully turned effusions and reflections.

There was nothing heroic about Gregory. To be just to him
one must study him as he was in his private life. There one per-
ceives, in spite of everything, a purity of intention, a delicacy
of moral feeling and, with all his introspectiveness, a genuine
sensitivity which remained capable of compassion and deep religious devotion to the end. Gregory's nature was extroverted
and declamatory, but he was not shallow and he knew as well
as Basil, and perhaps even better, the meaning of the spiritual
life.

He was at home in the same intellectual and social milieu as
Basil and many of his friends. He came from the same rich
nobility of Cappadocia which gave to the country its bishops
and to this ancient people a sudden and surprising impetus by
bringing them into touch with the Christian Faith and Greek
culture. Gregory also grew up in a Christian tradition. His
father, Gregory, had originally been a Hypsistarian, an adherent
of a hybrid Jewish-pagan sect which believed in the imageless
worship of the 'supreme' God; but his mother was a zealous
Christian and had secured her husband's conversion. He had
then been made bishop of the country town of Nazianzus.
Gregory was born not far from there, on one of his parents'
country estates at Arianzus, in 329–30. He was the ardently
longed-for late offspring of a marriage which had long been
childless and was, as he himself records, 'given up' and dedicated 'to the Lord' (Or. I, 77) by his mother from the very
beginning. The intensive religious education which he received
fell on fertile soil. Gregory never seriously pursued 'worldly'
ideals. He wanted to live wholly for the Saviour who had redeemed him, and he found the word of God 'sweeter than
honey'. But 'the world' in which he developed was no longer
a pagan world. With a voracious appetite the gifted youth
devoured all the cultural good things that were offered to him
in the schools of Caesarea in Palestine, in Alexandria, and above
all in Athens. In Athens he lived in a close and 'holy' fellowship

with Basil, who arrived there somewhat later. At that time
Gregory still thought of himself as the older and superior of the
two. He took his younger fellow-countryman under his wing,
introduced him to academic life, and tried to protect him from
the temptations of his environment. Inwardly, however, he
gave himself up to the intellectual delights of study with much
greater abandon than his quiet young friend. For Gregory intellectual culture, poetry, conversation, and art were life itself,
provided that the poisonous saps of paganism were drawn off
from the moral and aesthetic contents of classical literature and
that one was prepared to offer to Christ all the light and help
one gained from it. 'The wisdom of the Holy Spirit that comes
from above and derives from God, must rightly be the mistress
of all the lower kinds of culture' (*Carm. II, 2, 8 ad Seleucum*,
245 ff. This poem attributed to Gregory was probably written
by his younger cousin Amphilochius of Iconium; but it breathes
his spirit).

The term 'lower' culture used in this poem was meant entirely in the traditional sense of the word. Gregory took over
the cultural ideals of late antiquity, with its formalized rhetorical techniques and innumerable moral and philosophical plati-
tudes. But he also appropriated the classical texts, above all the
poetry of Homer and the tragedians, with lively enthusiasm and
with the assurance of the born orator, for whom it is a pleasure
to revive the old forms and apply them in a hundred different
ways. Gregory's knowledge of literature was unusually wide
and rich. He also had a philosophical training, but this did not
make him an independent thinker and scholar. He became a
rhetor. His numerous religious speeches and addresses were not
sermons on Biblical texts but oratorical masterpieces consisting
of official lectures, encomiums, memorial and funeral addresses
and addresses delivered on all kinds of ecclesiastical and personal
occasions. He can clearly be shown to have taken into account
the oratorical rules in the way he constructed his speeches and
developed his subject. He used in abundance the methods of
the contemporary 'Asian' style, comparisons and antitheses,

consonance and parallel rhythms, in mostly short sentences, displaying all the skill of the oratorical virtuoso. It is difficult for us to enjoy these much-admired addresses today. But they are thoroughly characteristic of Gregory's style. They surprise us by their constant and almost childlike self-centredness. Alongside the uninhibited description of the author's own character, opinions, and feelings, there is much self-praise but also self-accusation and extensive moralistic and psychological reflection. Nevertheless, they were intended to be spiritual and devotional works: they constantly introduce references to Biblical examples, words, and images, and everything is set in the light of eternity. They often close with a prayerful adoration of the Holy Trinity.

Needless to say, Gregory too attacked the Arian heresy in his addresses. He declared that the doctrine of God—that is, the orthodox confession of the Trinity—was the heart of the Christian Faith and of all true religion. In smooth, beautifully balanced formulas he unhesitatingly professed his faith in the essential unity of the three divine Hypostases. 'The Godhead is worshipped in the Trinity and the Trinity is gathered into a unity. It is worshipped as a whole and has royal power, sharing a single throne and a single glory, supramundane, supratemporal, uncreated, invisible, untouchable and incomprehensible, known only to itself as far as its inner structure is concerned, but worthy of our reverence and worship' (Or. VI, 22). 'To curtail the Trinity even a little is equivalent to destroying it completely, as though one were to make an assault on the doctrine of God altogether and with uncovered head' (Or. VI, 11). Gregory lays far more stress on the divine status of the Holy Spirit than did Basil, who hesitated to commit himself. For Gregory, with his Origenist training, the world of the spiritual and the spirit is the fundamental realm of religion. The Holy Spirit of God must liberate our spirit from its earthly fetters, and the ultimate goal of the Christian life is some day to become wholly divine.

No one was attacked and condemned by Gregory with such

anger and personal bitterness as the Emperor Julian the Apostate. Out of hatred for him, Gregory described his enemy, the 'Arian' Emperor Constantius, almost as a paragon of piety and virtue. Julian had issued the order which forbade Christians to be taught the classics. He was the worst kind of tyrant because he wanted 'to obstruct our education'; he was a hateful pioneer of folly because he hoped to triumph with unequal weapons in the struggle for the truth (*Or.* IV, 6). Gregory's personal interests were touched here. For him what he called 'Attic' education was a vital necessity and a vital element, and the more he failed to achieve a balance between the Attic and the Christian ideals at a deeper level, the more violently he protested when the classical values were turned against the Christian Faith. In his view the victory and the superiority of the Church would best be shown in its complete adoption of the traditions of classical culture. If Gregory sometimes acts as though he did not really care much for pagan wisdom, all that this indicates is a very slight sense of uncertainty. Such remarks need not be taken more seriously than the equally common and typically rhetorical assertion that his sole desire is to speak plainly and to the point, leaving on one side all the superficial brilliance of artificial eloquence. In fact he still regarded rhetoric as a 'weapon of virtue' in the hands of an honest man (*Or.* IV, 30).

Soon after Basil had left Athens, to devote himself again for a short time to the life of the world, Gregory decided to devote himself entirely to the 'theoretical' devotion and 'philosophy' of the monks: he made up his mind to go into quiet retreat. The exact dates are uncertain. This decision, he later remarked, might seem difficult to appreciate, but anyone who had ever been seized by the same longing would understand. It now seemed to him an incomparably wonderful thing 'to hold converse only with one's own self and with God' and to 'live one's life beyond the confines of the things one can see'. He wanted always to preserve 'these divine inspirations, unsullied by the impressions and the deceits of the world, and to be, and constantly to become afresh, a truly unblemished mirror of God

8

and the divine realities'. He wanted 'to add light to his light and receive brightness to replace the twilight, enjoying already by hope the blessings of the world to come; to have intercourse with the angels and, whilst sojourning on the earth, yet be taken away from it and be raised up to heaven by the Spirit' (Or. II, 7). It appears, however, that Gregory was not able to carry out his intentions. His parents wanted to have him with them in Nazianzus, and he was unable to leave them. He was baptized and in the end, at the request of the Church, consecrated presbyter by his own father. He must of course have given his consent in some way or other; all his complaints about having been forced into it and about his father's 'tyranny' cannot alter that (Carm. I, 1, 11 de vita sua 345). But he had hardly been ordained when he left the Church in protest, and retired to the Iris with Basil, to recuperate in solitude and to be inspired by his friend with new confidence and courage. He then returned and explained the reasons for his behaviour in no less than three pompous addresses. He had now, he declared, overcome his 'cowardice and weakness' (Or. I, 2). Fundamentally, they had only been the result of an overestimation of the spiritual office from which the pious were often the first to shrink back (Or. II). Now he had returned, but the congregation which had torn him away from his beloved solitude had not, unfortunately, responded to his sacrificial love with the love that was due in return and had thereby hurt him deeply (Or. III, 1-5). It is almost impossible to discover from these oratorical tirades and inflated private feelings what he really meant and what was behind the flow of words.

It was not long before the dogmatic conflicts began to beat upon Nazianzus. Gregory's own father had allowed himself to be misled into denying the Nicene Creed by signing the 'peace' formula which was laid before him. This led to disturbances in the Church in which monks took a leading part. But Gregory succeeded in inducing his father to make a new, orthodox declaration and to restore good relations. He also celebrated this event with a great speech. On the whole, Gregory had no liking for dogmatic quarrels, especially when they infected people outside the circle of expert theologians. He strove rather to appease than to incite the Church. He realized that there are limits to the desire for peace in Church affairs, but he did not believe in taking action out of mere distrust. 'Patience is better than rashness' (Or. VI, 20), and one must bear in mind those members of the Church whose faith is still not robust. The Church must express its orthodoxy 'not so much in words as in deeds' (Or. III, 7). Gregory's efforts for peace were purposeful and by no means fickle and unprincipled. But they do sometimes seem rather sentimental and personal. Even in church he was always speaking about his own feelings, his love for the Church and the worship of the common Father. This was connected with his deep need for friendship. He loved his younger brother Caesarius tenderly, and there was something ecstatic about his relationship with Basil. 'If I have gained anything from my life, it is my friendship and association with you!' (Ep. 58, 1 ad Basil). He was all the more deeply hurt by any difference of opinion with his friends or by any injustice, real or imagined, that was done to him.

Basil responded sincerely to Gregory's friendship but did not become infatuated. After he became Bishop of Caesarea ecclesiastical politics kept him very busy, and it is not surprising that he now tried to draw his friend Gregory into closer political association with him. Through the partition of the ecclesiastical province of Cappadocia, his power had been grievously weakened. He tried to fortify the fluctuating position of the Nicaeans by establishing new bishoprics. So Gregory should be made a bishop: the small, disputed frontier village of Sasima, in the neighbourhood of Nazianzus, should be kept loyal through him. This was a mistake. Basil should have taken into account his friend's character and limitations instead of making straight for the goal with his usual determined energy. At first, however, Gregory submitted and allowed himself to be consecrated (372). He began to resist violently only when the moment came to enter seriously upon the duties of his office. In the end he escaped to the mountains resentful, unhappy and depressed. He never took up his duties in Sasima, and years later his anger would break out when he came to speak of this episode. What presumption it was, he declared, to transplant him, Gregory, for purely political ends, to such a God-forsaken post town where no green leaf and no free man could thrive!

> The spiritual welfare of the faithful formed the pretext;
> but lust for power was the real reason—
> not to mention interest and tax money,
> for which the world tears itself to pieces.
>
> (*Carm. II, 1, 11, de vita sua 460 ff.*)

It is not an attractive spectacle, this attempt on Gregory's part to conceal his own failure by making the most unworthy charges against the dead friend whom he had always praised so highly. But it was his misfortune that he could never refuse the ecclesiastical tasks which were offered him, partly from a sense of duty and partly from vanity and weakness. If he had been more independent and less considerate he would have saved himself considerable embarrassment and many a painful exposure of his impotence.

This time too the pause for breath did not last long. For the second time Gregory was unable to withstand his father's fervent entreaties. He went back to Nazianzus to work as a kind of coadjutor until his father died, almost a hundred years old, in the year 374. Gregory refused to become his successor, and when his mother died too in the following year there was nothing to keep him in the desolate town so he retired to Seleucia in Isauria, where he pursued his intellectual and theological interests for a few years in the manner of an ascetic, conducting an extensive correspondence with his fellow Nicaeans throughout the world. They turned to him and he had to advise them. After the death of Basil, Gregory had become the leading authority for many of the young Nicaeans. But even now he was not happy. Although not yet fifty years old, he was lonely and exhausted. There is something moving about his hypochondriac complaints: 'You ask how I am,' he writes to a rhetor friend. 'Well, I am very bad. Basil I have no longer, Caesarius I have no longer; my spiritual and my physical brothers are both dead. "My father and mother have left me," I can say with David. Physically I am ill, age is descending on my head. Cares are choking me; affairs oppress me; there is no reliance on friends and the Church is without shepherds. The good is vanishing; evil shows itself in all its nakedness. We are travelling in the dark; there is no lighthouse and Christ is asleep. What can one do? I know only one salvation from these troubles, and that is death. But even the world to come seems terrible to judge by the present world' (*Ep. 80 ad Eudoxium:* this is the complete text of this beautifully written little letter).

In fact the great change for which Basil had striven all his life was now imminent, and it was to give Gregory another chance to act. It was to take him for the first time beyond the sphere of Asia Minor and put him for a brief while in the very centre of events in the Church.

The disaster of the Battle of the Visigoths at Adrianople (378), in which the Emperor Valens had lost his life, had had an important effect on the organization of the Church. Theodosius the Great, an orthodox Spaniard, had succeeded to the imperial throne, and the reformation of the Church in accordance with Nicene theology was now only a matter of time. The Emperor was still residing in the Latin West, but Gregory was already receiving from various quarters an invitation to accept the small Nicene church at Constantinople, which was without a pastor, so as to fill the vacuum in the capital city, which had been occupied by an Arian for the past forty years. To his followers, Gregory seemed the best, most representative man available for the post, and he accepted the appointment, under protest and from 'compulsion' as usual, but, all the same, he accepted it. This time a refusal would in fact have been justified on tactical grounds, in view of the risks involved in the obscure political situation then prevailing in the Church. One has the impression that Gregory had correctly appreciated the significance of the moment, for this time he really did apply his whole strength to the difficult task, and tackled it not without courage and skill. The next two years are the highlight of his life.

When this outwardly unimposing man appeared in Constantinople, the Nicaeans did not even have a church at their disposal. Gregory had to begin by holding services in a modest chapel, under threats of tumults and disturbances which for a time seriously endangered him. But he refused to be intimidated, and the great theological lectures which he began to deliver immediately provided just what was expected of him. They offered a brilliant and well-considered exposition of Nicene theology, lucid arguments with no descent to pettiness, and a firm exhortation to his tiny flock to set a worthy example in the practical life of the Church, which would stimulate all lovers of peace to join them. Gregory was clearly determined to maintain as far as possible a position above party struggle without surrendering his own dogmatic convictions and thus prepare in an effective way for his own appointment and the future reorganization of affairs.

His limited knowledge of human nature and lack of experience of ecclesiastical politics were already demonstrated in an incident which might have had serious consequences. One of the people who joined his church and tried to become particularly attached to Gregory was a certain 'philosopher' called Maximus, from Egypt, a Christian rhetor like Gregory himself. Gregory later derided him as a Cynic and an untruthful windbag who had been, with his golden dyed hair, an utterly trivial, idle fop and a shameless hypocrite. But to begin with he had apparently given him a warm welcome as a kindred spirit and, as was his habit, had immediately made a public speech about him. In fact the man was a rival in disguise who, as Gregory had been by the Nicaeans, had been marked out by the jealous patriarch of Alexandria as the future bishop and ordered to go to Constantinople. A premature attempt to have him consecrated brought the plot to light, and Maximus was forced to disappear. When Theodosius appeared in Constanti-

nople for the Christmas festival in the year 380 he found that
Gregory was the sole Nicene candidate. The Arian bishop, who
had ruled the city hitherto, was now summarily sent into exile
and Gregory was welcomed as his presumptive successor.
Under strong military escort he took possession of the Church
of the Apostles, at the side of the Emperor. But he did not yield
to the pressure to have him installed as bishop right away because he wanted stronger ecclesiastical backing. This was to
be provided by the Synod that met in the spring of the year
381.

The so-called second Ecumenical Council was attended, to
begin with, almost entirely by the young Nicene partisans of
Asia Minor and Syria. Everything therefore promised well.
Meletius of Antioch, who presided, had Gregory elected immediately. He was consecrated and enthroned and formally
installed as bishop of the capital. For the first time in his life he
appears not to have put up any serious resistance and showed
himself ready to accept the lustrous and responsible post. But
the opposition of the various groups and factions soon began
to make itself felt again. Shortly after Gregory's election,
Meletius died unexpectedly, and the old, unhappy dispute
about the occupation of the See of Antioch came once more
on the agenda (cf. p. 97). Gregory now hit upon the unfor-
tunate idea that the whole Antiochene Church should be
handed over to the former old Nicene candidate Paulinus. This
was in accordance with an earlier agreement and was now put
forward as a token of true justice and reconciliation, but politically it was impossible to put into practice. Gregory failed to
overcome the opposition of his own friends. In vain he used the
old method which he had applied after the Maximus affair, of
threatening to resign and take flight. He was compelled to
admit defeat. His position became really desperate when the
'Western' bishops, that is, first and foremost, the Egyptians,
appeared at the Council and set about him from the opposite
side. Gregory was unable to hold out any longer. He declared
that although he was innocent he wanted, like Jonah, to plunge

into the sea for the good of all, and he then announced his resignation, which was accepted. It was a bitter decision. His farewell address was dignified and saved his face, but it is not surprising to anyone who knows Gregory that on later occasions, especially in his great autobiographical poem, he gave vent to his profound annoyance and ill feeling and pulled to pieces the uneducated, narrow-minded bishops, the quarrelsome Council, and councils in general.

Once again, therefore, the old orator failed in an attempt to occupy an ecclesiastical post—this time even more painfully than usual, because he had really done his best and not reckoned on such an ending. To the outside world he repeatedly declared that he was only too glad to be away from the turmoil of the day-to-day struggle and be able to return to philosophical peace and quiet. But it took time for the wound to heal and before he could really enjoy his newly-won freedom. First he went back to Nazianzus, which was still without a bishop, and he took on the work there until he was able, after some difficulties, to appoint someone else as bishop. The new Christological heresy of the Apollinarians gave him much trouble at this period. In the end he retired to his father's estate at Arianzus, where for about seven years he really was able to live a life of leisure. He must have died in the year 389–90.

Gregory did not change in these last years of his life. He complained a great deal, criticized profusely, spoke and wrote incessantly about himself, his moods, and his sufferings. But the complete freedom with which he was now able to express himself made him seem more amiable, more natural, and also more serious than in his earlier years. Always a keen letter-writer, he now devoted himself to this most personal form of literature with special affection. As far as we know, he was the first Greek author to collect and publish his own letters. He also took up a new hobby: writing poetry in all possible classical meters. He wrote epigrams, surveys of past events, theological treatises, and, above all, 'about himself'. Much of his writing is simply prose turned into verse, like, for example, a poem on the differences between the family trees of Jesus as given by Matthew and Luke respectively. Other poems are more elegant and more personal, but even at their best his efforts do not amount to anything more than successful humanistic verse. Gregory's extensive classical education made it easy for him to find apt phrases, images, and similes for every mood and every thought. His writings are full of allusions and literary references. He believed that verse forced a writer to practise self-discipline. He wanted to prove that the new Christian culture was no longer inferior to paganism in this field. He apparently hoped for an even more immediate effect of his poems on the Apollinarians, who also, like the Arians, used verse in their propaganda. Above all he enjoyed the new opportunities his freedom gave him for literary activity and expression, now that his days as an orator were over.

> As an old man it has done me good
> to write verse and to sing to myself
> no lament, but a song of farewell
> like the old swan that whispers consolation
> to itself with its tired wings.
>
> (Carm. II, 1, 39, in suos versus 55 ff.)

Gregory expresses himself with the greatest simplicity, warmth, and directness whenever he speaks about those dear to him, his dead relatives and friends, and when he testifies to his faith in Redemption. We have already noted that as a Trinitarian theologian Gregory was not really creative, but merely completed and continued to defend in polished terms the position held by Basil. Much more important and revealing are his late anti-Apollinarian statements on the work and person of Christ. Apollinaris curtailed the human nature of Christ in order to strengthen his relation with the Godhead. Gregory was concerned to stress the complete humanity of the Saviour, alongside his complete divinity. Just as Christ's human nature and, particularly, his human spirit, the reality of which was denied by the Apollinarians, are raised wholly into the divine,

so our spirit is to be transfigured and deified through its association with Christ. Gregory is, however, not satisfied with this
spiritualistic conception of Redemption. Christ, the God-man
and the Lord, is indispensable to him above all because his holy,
unfathomable suffering and death have provided the atonement
by which the power of the devil and of sin, the whole burden
of our human failings, is truly overcome. It is as though in his
individualistic weakness and the disunity of his existence this
most delicate of the Church Fathers felt an irresistible need to
fix the final assurance of his salvation beyond all the 'vain'
human possibilities of religion, which otherwise meant so much
to him. In this respect Gregory perhaps went deeper than all
the Greek theologians before and after him. The nickname of
'the theologian' which was given him for his 'theological
addresses' in Constantinople was not wholly unjustified in a
deeper sense, though he owed his extraordinary reputation in
the succeeding age primarily to the formal qualities of his
writings, which were often used as models of style. It was the
orator, the 'Christian Demosthenes', as the Byzantines called
him, who had the strongest influence on posterity, not the
'theologian'. The real theologian, in the scholarly, 'philosophical' sense, was rather his namesake and occasional confidant, Basil's younger brother, Gregory of Nyssa.

CHAPTER IX

GREGORY OF NYSSA

GREGORY OF NAZIANZUS had regarded himself as dedicated to God from his youth onwards, but he had nevertheless remained, even as a Churchman and bishop, the rhetorician. Gregory of Nyssa came from the same intellectual and social world, and his friends probably took it for granted that he would devote himself to spiritual affairs and the clerical profession. By nature, however, he was not cut out to be a bishop. He was a thinker and a philosopher; he had a sharp, observant eye and an unusual talent for systematic thinking, but he was not a man for Church life and life in community. The energy which Basil used up in the outward service of the Church was, in Gregory, concentrated on intellectual pursuits, and he was not without ambition in this sphere of activity. That this man nevertheless became first a rhetor and then a bishop is typical of the age in which he lived. Culture was based on the rhetorical tradition, and the Church attracted to itself everything which helped in the development of the spiritual life. Gregory's life appears to differ according to whether it is examined from the outside or from the inside, and this gives him a difficult, problematical quality.

Although Gregory is usually described as timid and shy, he was perhaps originally not so unlike his brother Basil. Both felt the same need for independence, both had a conscious pride which was sometimes expressed rather contemptuously, and both were determined to develop their intellectual and spiritual personalities. Basil, however, voluntarily sacrificed these things, whereas Gregory had to struggle for the rights of his personality, had to fight for his position and way of life. He was burdened with the fate of the younger brother; he was the camp follower of a great generation, and he never acquired the certainty of a wholehearted surrender which gave such harmony to the character of Basil. Despite his outstanding cleverness, he long remained in the second rank, and in consequence there is a veiled, remote, and sometimes ambiguous quality about even his originality and his theology.

Admittedly, he too became very famous in the end, and occasional references which he made to it show that his fame gave him pleasure. As the brother of Basil the Great he was regarded as, with Gregory of Nazianzus, the man best qualified to preserve Basil's legacy, and on all dogmatic questions he was considered a leading authority. But, apart from his closest relatives, he had hardly any friends. His interesting correspondence is silent on this score. As a scholar and monk he lived his own life. He made supreme demands on himself, and his greatest achievements were in the fields of theology and philosophy. Basil had interpreted in his own way, given a Biblical depth to and tested in a new way the monasticism which Athanasius had won for the Greek world. Gregory followed him, but he gave to the ideal which he had taken over a different expression in the combination of reflection and meditation, and in the development of the basic ideas. He evolved and put his own stamp on a new theory of monastic, mystical piety which continued to live on.

For long stretches of time the outward course of his life is shrouded in darkness. He began to write only in his maturity, and it is impossible to reconstruct his previous development with any certainty. He must have been born *circa* 335. It seems that less money was spent on his education than on that of his elder brother Basil. We hear nothing about attendance at foreign universities, and Gregory himself confessed that he had nothing 'brilliant' to record about studying with famous teachers (*Ep. 13, 4 ad Liban.*). Again and again he pointed out that one man alone, Basil, had been his own 'teacher and father', and he praised him rapturously. For Gregory, Basil was 'the wonder of the whole world' and the prototype of the true philosopher (*Or. in XL Mart.*, Migne *Gr. 46, 776 A*); he sets him alongside the saints and declares that his writings are inspired. He was 'truly created according to the will of God and fashioned in his soul in the image of the Creator' (*De Hom. Opif.*, Migne *Gr. 44, 125 B*). His readers would perceive his dependence on Basil even where he does not refer to his teacher by name (*De Virg., Praef.*, Migne *Gr. 46, 320*). Gregory was indeed a pupil of Basil, but this rather deliberately fulsome praise does not mean at all that he stood still and had nothing independent to offer himself. The unconcerned way in which he 'makes the hard, refractory bread of Scripture' digestible by means of a free allegorical interpretation (*Hom. in Cant. 7,* Migne *Gr. 44, 925 B*) breathes a different spirit. Gregory must have read an unusual amount on his own, above all, Plato, Plotinus, and other Platonizing philosophers, and also Philo and, among Christian authors, Origen especially. He admired the pagan rhetor Libanius as the supreme living representative of classical Greek culture. Gregory was possibly the most versatile theologian of the century. His writings even contain discussions about natural science and medicine which reveal understanding as well as knowledge. In all this he was akin to Basil but undoubtedly superior even to him in the exhaustiveness and completeness of his knowledge.

In his youth Gregory had occasionally served as a lector. But he did not feel committed to this work. From sheer 'ambition', as Gregory of Nazianzus furiously declared in a letter, he allowed himself to be persuaded to exchange the Scriptures for the 'bitter and unpalatable books' of the world, to 'let himself be called more a rhetorician than a Christian' (*Greg. Naz. ep. 11 ad Greg.*). And he took a further step. He married Theosebia, a woman of high intellectual standing and greatly beloved. In his first treatise, *On Virginity*, he lamented that he could speak of this ideal only as a witness of the bliss that others experience, since he had himself once 'set his foot in worldly life' (*De Virg. 3*, Migne *Gr. 46, 325*). Such complaints should not be taken too seriously. Neither rhetoric nor the marriage, which he later conducted on a purely 'spiritual' level, obstructed his religious development. Gregory kept in touch with the monastic centre which his family maintained on the Iris, and he appears to have stayed there from time to time. His eldest sister, Macrina, the head of a nunnery there, was especially close to him. He called her his 'teacher' and devoted a little book to a moving account of her life and, in particular, of her death, at which he was present. Later on he composed a Dialogue, on the model of Plato's *Phaedo*, consisting of a conversation 'on the soul and the resurrection' which he claims to have had with his sister at this last meeting on earth.

At that time Gregory had long since given up his free life as a rhetorician and philosophizing theologian and had become bishop of the little town of Nyssa (in 371). From a life of personal culture, study, and contemplation he too had in the end been called to the service of the Church, by a way which he himself once described as the best and the most useful approach to ecclesiastical office. It appears that here too Basil had exerted his influence. As in the case of Gregory of Nazianzus, the place which was to be upheld by the appointment of Basil's brother was relatively modest in itself but politically important. Gregory of Nyssa also had to be 'compelled' forcibly to accept the post (*Basil Ep. 225 ad Demosth.*). He resigned himself to the new role, however, and soon began to take a more zealous part in ecclesiastical politics than was agreeable to Basil. The particulars are not quite clear. It is possible that Gregory maintained contact with the old Nicaeans with whom Basil had broken off relations, without admitting the deviation quite candidly. We have an unusually violent letter in which Basil even accuses Gregory of having forged certain letters and thereby brought about an extremely embarrassing situation. He said he would henceforth refuse to allow Gregory to take part in ecclesiastical negotiations; it had been proved that his words did not correspond to the facts. He flatly refused when it was suggested to him that Gregory should be sent to Rome as a legate; his brother was, he declared, quite inexperienced in ecclesiastical affairs and ill suited for such missions on account of his straightforward nature. Yet Gregory was equally under the pressure of the anti-Nicene régime and was affected even more directly than Basil himself, whom the State did not dare to touch. Accused of financial irregularities, he was deposed and an Arianizing bishop was put in his place. All the protests which Basil made to the governor were in vain: Nyssa was lost and Gregory was suspended and had to go abroad. He was able to return only after the great change that occurred in the year 378, when he was given a great ovation by his congregation. He took part in the Council of Constantinople in 381. By this time the brother of the great Basil, who was now no longer among the living, had become well known to a much wider public. By a decree issued by Theodosius the Great, he was appointed central bishop of the whole diocese of Pontus, which means that, in spite of the unimportance of his ecclesiastical position, he was made confidential adviser to the government and he had the last word in the matter of removing Arians and appointing new Nicene bishops. Even before this we find Gregory attending foreign synods. He travelled by the State post to Arabia and visited Jerusalem; he conducted the election of the Bishop of Ibora in Armenia Minor and only just escaped being elected Bishop of Sebaste himself. In the story of her life he made Macrina say that his fame now outshone that of his ancestors, his name was mentioned in cities, churches, and among the nations, and 'churches call and send for him, that he may stand by them in their struggle to create order' (*Vita Macr.*, Migne Gr. 46, 981 B).

Nevertheless, Gregory remained a difficult colleague to work with, and with his critical comments was far from universally popular. He summed up his impressions of the Holy Land in a letter which represents an outright attack on conditions in that country. 'I know perfectly well what people will say in reply' (*Ep. 2, 11 ad Censit.*), but it is a fact that disorder, depravity, and immorality nowhere thrive so greatly as in the great centres of pilgrimage. Genuine piety is now more at home among the

Cappadocians. People should be dissuaded from going on pilgrimages—on grounds of principle. The truly holy, philosophical life seeks for quietness and solitude; God does not limit his presence to holy places. If the spirit blows where it listeth, we shall share in his gifts by faith—'according to the proportion of faith' (Rom. xii. 6) and not 'according to the proportion of our physical stay in Jerusalem'. Gregory did not succeed in establishing a tolerable relationship with his own metropolitan. The latter's jealousy for his more famous subordinate, who was also the brother of his predecessor, may have had something to do with this failure.

In later years Gregory was twice again invited to Constantinople. He was asked to deliver funeral orations for members of the imperial family. In the year 394 he took part in a synod for the last time. He must have died soon afterwards. The fragmentary information which we have about him hardly suffices to build up a complete picture of his life, though it does suggest the unusual aspects of his character. To get to know Gregory properly, one has to concentrate on his theology and his writings.

It would be quite wrong to regard Gregory, with his self-willed and critical manner, as a sceptic or even a deliberately unecclesiastical theologian. Theologically he stands on the foundation of Mother Church, and his political activity suffices to show how unhesitatingly he recognizes and defends its public and sacred rights. The days of Clement of Alexandria were long past; there was no longer any theology which could develop in a purely academic atmosphere. The worship of the Church occupies a large space in his writings and sermons; he emphasizes the importance of the rule of law and the redeeming action of the sacraments, especially Baptism. He was the first Christian theologian clearly to define the concept of the priest, emphasizing the sacramental transforming power of his consecration and his distinguishing role of liturgist. To that extent he was a direct forerunner of the Areopagite, who, a century later, was to develop his momentous doctrine of the heavenly and ecclesi-

astical 'hierarchies'. But the Church's doctrine and 'philosophy'
are the all-important thing, and Basil's reserved way of keeping
within the bounds of the Bible on these matters was fundamentally alien to Gregory. In his methodical approach, he goes
back rather to Origen. He regards the preaching of the Church
merely as a starting-point for more advanced ideas, and the
intellectual consistency and logical foundations of the coherent
system are more important than proving its bases in the Scriptures. The teaching of the Church was now much more strongly
articulated and established than hitherto, and Gregory was careful to respect it and avoid all open resistance. Basically, however, he revived the old Gnostic scheme of theology as an
interpretation and development of a huge temporal and supratemporal drama in which, once removed by the Fall from
its original unity and God-relatedness, the spiritual being is
returning by broad, laborious ways to its origin. The fantastic
elements now recede into the background and the philosophical
interpretation of the mythology is more rigorously carried
through. The mythological elements are now interpreted from
a more strictly philosophical standpoint. In this respect Gregory
is still nearer to Plotinus than to Origen. On the other hand,
however, speculation is never regarded as an end in itself; like
ethics and natural philosophy and the whole of secular culture,
it has 'only to adorn the divine temple of mysterious revelation' (De Vita Moysis, Migne Gr. 44, 360 C). Christ stands at
its centre, and the real issue is the redemption of man, that is,
the elevation, purification, and return of the individual soul to
its Creator and Lord. Gregory seeks for a living relationship
with God, not a neutral order of graduated being. He does not
believe that there is any permanence in human nature; it can be
understood and truly realized only on the basis of its divine
destiny. Theology ends in the worshipping, loving union with
God who is incomprehensible and unfathomable. Everything
that takes place between created and uncreated being is conceived in terms of grace, and is fulfilled in the realm of freedom
and sanctification. Here is the dividing line between Christianity

9

and Neoplatonic pantheism. Gregory is fond of speaking of the deification of man, but he means the likeness unto God which man is called to attain, as an animated mirror cleansed from all the mire and rust of an earthly being, as the true image of God. For all eternity the one goal of man and blessedness itself is to be illumined and sustained by God. And it is the magnanimity of God, not our work, which alone permits and makes possible this homecoming and fulfilment.

In the years when he held a leading position in ecclesiastical politics, Gregory also occupied himself with the current controversies regarding the Trinity and the nature of Christ. In a number of treatises directed against the Arian Eunomius, he defended the orthodox doctrines of the Church with acumen, shrewdness, and accuracy. Gregory was more interested than Basil in the inner unity and permanent co-operation of the three divine Hypostases. He strove to relate the Spirit not only to the Father but also to the Son and he already broached the later problems of Western 'realism', that is, the problem of the real content of general concepts in their relation to concrete individuation. He also came to grips with Apollinarianism. Unlike Gregory of Nazianzus, he advocated a Christology which comes near to the later 'Antiochene' conception, in so far as a sharp distinction is made between the divine and the human nature in the person of the Saviour. In the 'Great Catechism' he dealt with the doctrine of the Trinity and the doctrines of the Incarnation and the Redemption, ending with Baptism, Communion, Faith, and Rebirth. The work was conceived as an aid to apologetic preaching; but in spite of its somewhat popular form it was the first major attempt since Origen to expound the whole teaching of Christianity as a unity. What moves Gregory most deeply, however, are not the topics of traditional theology, but the problems of man. The realization of salvation, the elevation and transformation of the individual, the relation to the life of the body and the survival of the soul after death—these are problems to which he returns again and again, however circuitously. They bridge the gap between his Platonic-Origenistic view of the world and the possibilities of personal moral development and education. In this connection the practical experiences of the philosopher-monk were useful and he probably drew also on more obscure sources, hidden in his own interior life. Gregory was a good and therefore, in the final analysis, a very discreet psychologist.

His early treatise *On Virginity* is already of interest from this point of view. Gregory, the Churchman and a married man, refuses to condemn marriage and its joys summarily, and he knows how to describe them vividly. However, only the life of chastity can really do justice to man's ultimate destiny, life in the freedom and power of the absolute holiness which embraces the soul as well as the body. All-destroying death lurks behind all the joys of the earth and the senses. Abiding life is to be found only in the spirit, which rises above the world. This raises at once the difficult problem of the meaning of the life of the body. It cannot simply be evil, but it is indissolubly bound up with sin. Gregory believes that it was created for us by God for the sake of later sin. But what happens when the soul leaves the body? What is its manner of existence between its individual death and the final, general resurrection? How is it possible for the body to receive back from the world the various elements belonging to it? What becomes of the organs of nourishment and reproduction which the sexless soul no longer needs? For a long time Gregory strives with acute, almost scientifically precise reflections to keep away from Origen's dangerous spiritualism. He partly revives the earlier criticisms directed against Origen. In the end, however, he accepts the pure spirituality of the heavenly body. After long detours he returns to an only slightly modified form of Origenism.

The soul, and the soul alone, is created in the image of God and for eternal communion with him. What this means is described by Gregory in glowing colours far surpassing the corresponding descriptions in Philo and Origen. Gregory was the founder of a new mystic and ecstatic piety. The progressive asceticism which he required of his monks is no mere exercise on the way to a future goal but leads to a loving encounter and union between Christ and his Church, between the soul and its God in the present. According to Gregory's allegorical interpretation, all of the Scriptures are concerned with these spiritual experiences. Whether it is a matter of Old or New Testament texts, of the 'Life of Moses' or the example of the Apostle Paul, he finds the same ideals, of purification, miraculous sanctification, and blessed communion with God. In particular, the Song of Solomon is made to bear fruit in mystical piety. The purified soul, full of the intoxication of sanctified sobriety, feels in the bright darkness of the divine night the approach and the beauty of its bridegroom, although, or rather because, he is always in part invisible, intangible and inexhaustible. 'Blessedness, says the Lord (Matt. v. 8), does not consist in knowing about God, but having God in oneself' (Or. de Beat. 6, Migne Gr. 44, 1269 C). To have God within, the soul must, like Christ, have already died to the world. 'If it does not die, it remains entirely dead; only through dying, and putting off everything mortal, can it attain to life' (Hom. in Cant. 12, Migne Gr. 44, 1020 B). The soul is always journeying on a yearning yet blissful 'journey to God, which can never end' (Hom. in Cant. 12, Migne Gr. 44, 1025 D), in a most wonderful unity of peace and movement. The waters of the liberated soul rush on to God like a fountain; 'it has the depth of the fountain, but the constant movement of the river' (Hom. in Cant. 11, Migne Gr. 44, 977 C). It is itself filled by God as by a stream; it is kindled by the light like a torch and borne aloft by the spirit as by a carriage. Whoever has experienced this will transmit what he has learned, as the prophets and apostles have done. The Church extends increasingly and the great upward movement of spirits is irresistible. Belief in the restoration of all to God is to be found in the end in Gregory as in Origen. For him too this is no cold metaphysical proposition. It is a confession of belief in the living experience of the Spirit who is God himself and therefore the ultimate royal power and victorious reality over and above all things.

Gregory was never condemned by name for this heresy. But the condemnations of the fifth and sixth centuries naturally had him in mind. Gregory defended his theses more boldly than the other Origenists of his age. At the same time, however, he stressed their hypothetical character, and he probably considered that the doctrine of the last things did not pertain to the dogmatic centre of theology but to questions the discussion of which should remain open and on which, as his friend Gregory of Nazianzus said, even an error is quite 'undangerous' (Greg. Naz. Or. 27, 10). This distinction is very characteristic. On the one side there is the doctrine of God as a universally binding, rigidly fixed dogma and, on the other, free mystic speculation fed from other sources which nevertheless touches on the most burning problems of personal life and faith. The intention seems to have been to remove or relax the tension between the individual and the Church as an all-sustaining whole. Basil had already been guided by such considerations in his ecclesiastical politics. The dogmatic tradition was becoming a power with which the theologian had to reckon. It was at this period that the first theological 'Florilegia' came into being, that is, collections of quotations from the older, recognized teachers of the Church for practical use in controversies about the valid truth. Gregory not only accepts with a new kind of emphasis everything the Scriptures say but also the guiding 'explanations of the Fathers' (Contra Eunom. III, 10, 9). 'It is enough for the proof of our doctrine that the tradition has come down to us from the Fathers, like an inheritance which was handed down from the apostles by the saints who came after' (Contra Eunom. III, 2, 98). Gregory appeals in the same vein to his older brother Basil the Great, but he does not go the whole way with him. He deviates into his own realms of thought and spiritual life, where he feels unconstrained and free.

CHAPTER X

SYNESIUS OF CYRENE

STRICTLY speaking, the man to whom this chapter is devoted
was not one of the recognized Fathers of the Church. He was
a marginal figure and an outsider, although his writings were
eagerly read and used and even commented on in the Byzantine
Middle Ages. It is true that Synesius was a philosopher, which
at this period meant also a theologian, but he was a pagan
rhetorician and aesthete, not a Christian. Nevertheless he was
made a Christian bishop toward the end of his life. That this
was possible is very revealing. The course of Synesius's life and
development confirms in a surprising way what has already
emerged in the last few chapters concerning the comprehensive
character of the Christian Church, attracting and uniting all the
intellectual forces of the time. It shows how broad had become
the stream which bore its life and teaching. There was a close
affinity between the last of the pagan philosophers and the
Fathers of the Church. There was on both sides the same element of spiritual inwardness and devout speculation, the same
striving after moral purity and sanctification, the same reverence for the treasures of revelation, culture, and knowledge
which the ancient traditions held for those who were prepared
to learn. There was ultimately, however, only one organization
in which these ideals could be put into practice and find a
socially responsible expression: the great Catholic Christian
Church. In the end, even the recalcitrant and even the pagans
found their way to its portals.

In this respect Synesius may be compared with the great
Cappadocians. His homeland, Cyrenaica, was originally a 'barbaric' region which had been opened up to Hellenistic culture
and Roman order at an earlier date and even more thoroughly

than Cappadocia. Here too there was a rich, land-owning nobility, and Synesius was a member of one of the oldest families in the area, which traced its descent back to a companion of Herakles. Like the Cappadocians, he combined Hellenistic cosmopolitanism and the imperial outlook with a vigorous and assured patriotism which was rural and provincial rather than urban and bourgeois in character. He too had a deep sense of family. He cultivated friendships and spent much of his time in social intercourse. To all who came to him he gave his generous help. For him, too, Platonism—in his case, pagan Platonism—implied a philosophical obligation which was also, in the full sense of the word, religious. He strove to spend his whole life as it were under the eyes of the one omnipotent God and never tired of praising and adoring his glory. His piety was lacking, however, in the monastic and ascetic features which gave to the faith of his Christian contemporaries a far more impassioned but also a more violent and tortured quality. Synesius gives an impression of wholeness, harmony, and purity. In his writings, too, he is quite open and natural and unaffected. His writings are, he says, his children which he has begotten partly with philosophy, partly with the poetry that is worshipped in the same temple, and partly with the rhetoric of the times. 'But one can see that they are all children of the one father who has sometimes given himself up to the most serious effort and at others to cheerful pleasure' (*Ep. 1, 1 ad Nicand.*). In the philosophical style of his late period Synesius is fond of reflecting on his ideals and way of life, but he is not so obtrusively vain as many other pagan sophists, and a man like Gregory of Nazianzus among the Fathers of the Church. He is concerned to defend his cheerful versatility against the attacks of cantankerous critics, and appeals on this score to Dio Chrysostom, of Prusa, the philosophical world citizen of the first century A.D., his ideal example. Why should he too not be allowed to alternate freely between theory and practice, between philosophical and artistic pursuits, and nevertheless be a complete philosopher?

The culture and reading of this unpedantic man are amazing. He has the whole of Greek literature at his command—philosophers, poets, orators—and in his fervent admiration for the 'classical' tradition he reminds one of the early humanists. He writes a faultless, carefully polished Attic, though he writes his hymns, appropriately, in the Doric dialect. He seems to be able to turn his hand to anything; he will quote and imitate and then write quite freely in his own style. He wrote tracts and reports, speeches, poems, occasional pieces, letters, and diaries. But the impression he leaves is that not of the trained writer but rather of the superior aristocrat and master of the art of life who has everything well under control. He does not evade the political obligations of his social position. 'Books and the chase are my life—when I am not on a mission' (*De Insomn.* 18). He loved his quiet country estate of Anchemachos as Basil had loved his monastic homestead on the Iris. But his studies did not exclude military and equestrian exercises, for which he had a 'wild passion' from his young days (*Ep. 105 ad Fratrem* [Hercher p. 706]). The philosophy of such a man is bound to be an eclectic construction, but it should not be condemned as mere dilettantism, for it permeated his whole life and was based on the foundation of a serious education.

Synesius studied in Alexandria, the great cultural metropolis. He had the good fortune to be introduced to the world of the mind not merely by the purely academic route: in Hypatia, the greatly admired Neoplatonist who taught philosophy, he found a teacher who charmed and inspired him and became a lifelong friend. At the same time he entered a circle of like-minded young people and later found a wife in a distinguished Christian family living in the city. One is reminded of the intellectual friendship which Basil and Gregory of Nazianzus—no less hungry for culture, and enthusiasts for Platonism—began in Athens. Synesius later visited Athens but it disappointed him, in comparison with Alexandria. In his opinion, only the famous name and the 'husk' of its former life remained. Philosophy had long since vanished from it and 'changed its quarters'. 'In our time the soil of Egypt is developing the seeds which Hypatia sowed there' (*Ep. 136* [*135*] *ad Fratrem* [Hercher p. 722]).

Unfortunately, the information we have about the teaching of this unusual woman is only indirect and incomplete. She was an austere scholar yet impressed everyone, even the populace of Alexandria, as a personality. Synesius was introduced to the foundations of ancient culture and all his life retained a keen interest in astronomy in particular. But everything was ultimately fused in a great Neoplatonic system in which the ideas of Porphyry were revived. The ultimate 'mysteries' of this school hardly became public knowledge because it was decidedly pagan and did not dare come into conflict with the laws of the Christian State.

The study of nature and its mysterious forces led to a higher knowledge of the intellectual and spiritual world, which led back by degrees to the divine One who is reflected in the whole cosmos but can be worshipped worthily only in a state of vision and adoration which transcends the whole visible world. What this conception meant to Synesius is seen perhaps most vividly in a little treatise which continues to arouse interest even today: the treatise on dreams which the author claimed to have written in the early hours of a single night. What a wonderful realm of beauty, knowledge, and revelation dreams open up to every human being! No particular place of worship, no tricks are needed. It was not Synesius's intention to write a popular book of dreams and oracles. In dreams the soul is released from its material confines. In the power of imagination it stirs its wings and approaches the source of its true being. Admittedly, there is in dreams the danger of deception and seduction according to the inner condition of the dreaming soul. But a holy spirit, purified by moderation and discipline, quickly leaves behind these demonic possibilities and the theurgic experiments of manticism. It rises, light and dry, on the wings of divine grace to the types of the eternally true and real and comes to know the supreme reality: the suprasensual essence, the bright eternal meaning of spiritual things, and its own natural rights in a world which no time can destroy. When interpreted aright, the world of dreams testifies to the intellectual-sympathetic unity of the world beneath its chaotic surface and proves the immortality of the soul. This is admittedly no pabulum for a half-educated public. The 'teachers of the people' in the cities who, encouraged by their own lack of education, disputed about God with everyone, would have liked to gain the allegiance of Synesius; but he adhered to the judgment of Hypatia alone (*Ep. 154 ad Philos. Magistr.* [Hercher p. 735]). He kept his distance from and thereby expressed his contempt for the 'Christian philosophy' of the proselytizing bishops, but he did the same in regard to certain pagan 'sophists'. He wanted to remain independent of all parties and faithful only to the supreme truth known to man.

Soon after his return home Synesius had to participate in a far-reaching undertaking of his fellow-citizens. Seriously damaged by the repeated incursions of desert tribes, cruelly exploited by incompetent officials and only inadequately defended, the province needed a remission of taxation which could be obtained only at the imperial court itself. Synesius undertook this mission, and it was to keep him in Constantinople for three years, which he later recalled as horrible, lost years which he would much rather have spent at home with his 'books and the chase'. Even so, they were not without influence on his development. The rich, intellectually outstanding notability now became at home in the highest society. He learned how to make his way in the labyrinth of court diplomacy; he made influential connections and found admirers and recognition. Synesius was allowed to make a speech 'About the Empire' before the young Arcadius and his court. Despite its conventionally rhetorical style, it expresses certain features of his character and outlook. Synesius not only summoned the courage to protest against corruption and the abuse of power but made himself the spokesman of the anti-Goth movement. He declared that it was a disgrace that the defence of the frontiers and the most important administrative posts in the Empire were being transferred to the barbarians, the ravenous wolves, instead of the 'watchdogs' prescribed by Plato. He lived to see a change in favour of the national 'Roman' court clique. Synesius described the change in the mystifying language of a treatise entitled *The Egyptians or: On Providence* which records the fall and the return of his patron, the City Prefect Aurelian, who appears in the mask of Osiris, who has been persecuted by his evil brother Typhon. This is a work that tries to be philosophical, mythical, and historical at one and the same time, and is typical of the Baroque taste of 'society' at that period. Another little treatise of this time describes an ingenious astronomical instrument which Synesius presented to a highly placed personality. To appreciate his humorous side, one should read the 'adoxographical' joke, *In praise of Baldness* (*Calvitii Encomium*)—another typical example of rhetorical improvisation but executed with the utmost elegance.

It may reasonably be doubted whether Synesius was well advised, in the long run, to protest against the allegedly destructive and unnecessary German troops. But he was still a genuine romantic nationalist, for he matched his words with deeds. When he returned home he immediately attempted to organize the frontier guard. He put a strong militia force on its feet, took the field himself, invented a new missile, and strengthened the frontier fortifications against the 'barbarians'. He co-operated with the government commanders and officials, often gave them instructions, and where they were obvious failures replaced them. Once again, Platonism was making practical demands and inspiring political activity. As soon as peace was achieved, Synesius returned to his 'philosophical' life. We find him on his country estate among his books and writings, with his friends and occupied with the education of his nephew. He sings the praise of leisure, of study, spiritual devotion and composure, and he also sings the praises of God's glory. The hymns which we have already mentioned represent the finest and most solemn expression of this mood.

Synesius's hymns are carefully elaborated works of art composed in all possible classical rhythms, full of literary allusions, but also full of bold linguistic innovations. They are genuine religious lyrics, 'philosophical' lyrics of radiant majesty, based on the doctrines of the Neoplatonic philosophers. Admiration for the beauty of the cosmos, prayerful ascent to the inexpressible One, the soul's yearning for purity and perfection, are expressed in a stream of high emotion.

> Unto the King of Gods our voice we raise:
> To him a crown we weave, and bring
> A sacrifice of words, a bloodless offering.
>
> (Hymn. 1 [3], 8–11)

Spiritual praise has taken the place of the old devotional conventions, which the law forbids and which the philosophical man of prayer no longer needs. Probably the nine hymns were written in the period before Synesius was made a bishop and before he became a member of the Church. Nevertheless, Christian concepts already appear alongside purely pagan and mythological conceptions. One of the hymns obviously extols Christ's descent into hell and his Ascension; in another the author has in mind the adoration of the Magi. One senses a progressive approximation to the specifically Christian in the constant stream of feeling. The divine 'offspring' and 'hero' is transformed into the 'Logos', the 'Son', and the 'Son of the Virgin'; the Neoplatonic triad of the One, the Creative Mind, and the World Soul becomes the threefold power of the Christian Trinity. But it is questionable how far one should evaluate the hymns in this way as personal confessions and interpret them biographically. Synesius senses the affinity of the images and concepts, he does not scruple to use the Christian 'mythos', and he pays homage to its truth. For him, paganism and Christianity stand alongside one another like two related 'denominations', and the truth which they share is greater than that which divides them. The poet who lives with a Christian wife in the happiest of marriages differs from the Christian view of life on quite a number of points and is not inclined to join the Church. But that does not prevent him from paying his tribute to the truth in all the forms in which it appears. His letter to a Christian friend who has been converted to monasticism is typical (*Ep. 147* [*146*] *ad Johann.*). In themselves the coarse 'blackcoats' (monks) are not very attractive to Synesius, but he has no desire to cast doubts on the seriousness of their contemplative life and he heartily congratulates his friend for having attained with a single step what he has striven and is still striving after for so long in his white philosopher's mantle. 'I praise everything that happens for the sake of the Divine.'

That is the position of the man who was elected Bishop of Ptolemaïs in the summer of the year 410, and thereby became the leading cleric in the whole of Cyrenaica. To understand how this happened it must be remembered that at this time a bishop was legally and traditionally the most important and influential person in public life and was by no means restricted in his activities to the purely religious sphere. He was the man in whose hands the tasks of social welfare and to some extent the administration of justice converged, the only speaker whom no one could prohibit from speaking, the champion of the oppressed against the arbitrary actions of the tax official and the political bureaucracy. It is no accident that higher officials were often transferred to an important episcopal post. How much a vigorous metropolitan can achieve and signify is shown by the life of Basil and of any great bishop in our own time. It was therefore quite natural for the Christians of Cyrene to want to put in charge of their ecclesiastical administration the most energetic and influential feudal lord of their country who was also the most outstanding man intellectually, as well as the richest.

Did Synesius wish to be elected or was he taken by surprise? In his intimate letters he later emphasized more than once that acceptance of the appointment was a great sacrifice, that he would rather have died a thousand deaths than bear the burden of such an office, and he appeals to the 'God who honours philosophy and friendship' to testify that he is telling the truth (*Ep. 96* [*95*] *ad Olymp.* [Hercher p. 691]). He explains that an obstinate refusal would have made life impossible; he could only accept the office or renounce his beloved homeland. Such utterances are perfectly credible, but a man of his kind cannot be judged solely by the criterion of his own feelings. Once before Synesius had been considered a possible candidate for a political office, and at the time he had declared himself ready not to refuse—although he was not really cut out for that kind of appointment. He now had to face the problem a second time and in a new and more serious form, and it appears that he considered it in just the same light as before: the fatherland needed him, and Synesius could and would not wantonly evade the service required of him. The decision that he now had to make was, however, no longer a purely external one. The bishop is also the moral and religious leader and teacher of his people. He should represent publicly what true philosophy demands. It was just this responsibility which evidently made such an impression on Synesius. He regarded the call to office as no mere accident: it was not man but God himself who demanded this service of him. And 'with him, it is said, all things are possible, even the things that otherwise seem impossible' (*Ep. 11 ad Presb.* [Hercher p. 648]).

On the other hand, however, the difficulties were also quite obvious. Synesius had never been baptized and was not a Christian. He did not feel able simply to disown his previous convictions. He did not want to arouse any false hopes. Above all, his future superior, Bishop Theophilus of Alexandria, who would have to consecrate him, would have to be told beforehand in all frankness what he would be doing. The way out of the dilemma which Synesius chose was to explain his views at great length in a letter to his brother, clearly stating the things he would and would not be prepared to do if appointed. This letter was intended, as he emphatically pointed out, to be read by everyone and to make the situation clear to the patriarch. It was therefore a very carefully conceived 'open letter', every word of which was important (*Ep. 105, ad Fratrem*).

'It would', the letter begins, 'be extremely difficult to understand if I were not very grateful to the citizens of Ptolemaïs for considering me worthy of a task which I am unable to believe myself capable of undertaking'. The dignity of this new spiritual office requires an utterly composed, immaculate soul of priestly sanctity, and Synesius is far from being satisfied that he is worthy. A declaration of one's own unworthiness is the usual procedure in such cases, but Synesius underlines the conventional statement with a reference to his previous, thoroughly secular life, so unsuitable as a preparation for the life of a public teacher of the laws of God. Synesius is, however, clearly prepared to make the sacrifice required of him, for the sake of the cause. The joys of the chase, of sport, and even of private study will have to cease. But he is not prepared to give up his marriage. In his view it would be equally wrong to part entirely from his wife or to maintain his relationship with her in secret. 'On the contrary, I want many, well-bred children.' Synesius no longer has any hesitation about joining the Church and accepting baptism: that is a precondition of episcopal office which he now takes for granted. More important are a number of reservations on dogmatic matters which he is careful to make quite clear. He will have to be allowed to conceive the Faith in philosophical terms, and where the barriers between his beliefs and current ecclesiastical dogmas are insurmountable he will have to be allowed to remain loyal to his previous views. The eternity of the world, the pre-existence of the soul, belief in its immortality and not in physical resurrection were some of the points of difference on which he refused to yield. Synesius was prepared, however, not to attach too much importance to them. He should not be expected to contradict them and in private he should be allowed to remain a philosopher; but he would 'speak mythologically' in public, as required of him. For a Neoplatonist an offer of this kind was not treason. He knew that the ultimate truths about the Divine should not in any case be revealed to the masses. Nevertheless, as a bishop he would never say anything but what he thought, since God and sincerity belong together.

The purpose of the letter is obvious: Synesius wants to make it impossible for him to be reproached later on or for action to be taken against him for heresy. If his conditions are accepted, he is willing to be consecrated. Unfortunately, we do not know how the decisive negotiations with the patriarch proceeded. Synesius had known Theophilus from the time of his sojourn in Alexandria; Theophilus had even solemnized his marriage. He can hardly have been very happy about this letter and the situation that it created. He of all men should not have been prepared to consider such proposals, having set himself up as the strong man of faith in the fight against heretics and Origenists. But evidently he did not like to refuse; he did not want to incur the displeasure of either the celebrated candidate himself or the province of Cyrene, which lay at the outer edge of his province. We only learn that Synesius stayed no less than seven months in Alexandria before returning as a consecrated Christian bishop. Possibly he agreed to renounce his marriage in the end, for his wife is never mentioned in the subsequent period. It should certainly not be assumed, however, that Synesius sacrificed his philosophical convictions. Not a word of the open letter that he had issued was withdrawn and it remained in force.

The picture we get of the activities of Bishop Synesius is all the more astonishing. Although he had refused to surrender his convictions, he appears to have been in every respect a loyal, conscientious, and completely orthodox bishop, differing outwardly not at all from his Catholic colleagues. We see him travelling about his diocese, settling disputes, founding monasteries, conducting ordinations. He submits queries to his patriarch, seeks for spiritual counsel from the holy monk Isidorus of Pelusium, and where a heresy such as that of the radically Arian Eunomians appears he takes vigorous action against it. The fragments of his sermons that have survived are of irreproachable doctrinal correctness, and he now quotes from the Bible with a zeal and accuracy which were quite alien to him earlier on, compared with his knowledge of Plato and the old poets.

All this was required of him by the service which he undertook, to lead the people and to lead them to the worship of God. Synesius did not change his faith: he merely translated into the forms prescribed by public life the attitude which he had cherished throughout his life as a philosopher and a private individual.

It goes without saying that Synesius did not cease to participate in the political struggles of his homeland. More than ever before he set all the machinery in motion to prevent a military disaster in the struggle with the desert tribes. The situation had worsened and at times seemed almost desperate. Synesius was determined to hold out to the last. He refused to take flight, but if all resistance should prove in vain he was ready to embrace the columns of the altar and await the final blow in church. Even now he sees to the enlistment of recruits and all the measures which can be taken for the defence of the country. He makes impassioned appeals to the public. But he now has even more effective weapons at his disposal for use against the disloyalty of those responsible for the country's weakness. The first excommunication of which we hear in the history of the Church was imposed by Synesius on the Duke Andronicus who had been responsible for a great many cases of blackmail and brutality. A notice went out to the sister churches throughout the world stating that he and his accomplices must be barred from every house of God and that all who shared a roof or a table with him were to incur the same dire penalty. Synesius forced the proud criminal to repent and brought him to heel. Who would have suspected the gentle Neoplatonist of former days to be capable of such medievally stern action?

Yet Synesius had not really changed. He suffered unspeakably from the tasks and burdens he had to bear. He complained that everything had changed and the pleasure, honour, and happiness that formerly filled his life had gone. In his family affairs too he was dogged by serious misfortune. His brother had to escape from the country to avoid being elected *Decurio*, that is, the public guarantor of the receipt of taxes, a post which

10

would have ruined him financially. Synesius saw his three beloved sons die one after the other, and the grief broke his heart.
But in public he proudly repressed all his private suffering and
gave vent to his complaints only in occasional, brief notes to
his old friends. He believed that it was not for nothing that the
dream oracle prophesied that death would come in the year of
his accession to office. He felt as though he were dead already.
One of his last letters, full of grief and weariness, was addressed
to Hypatia, his 'lady' and teacher. Soon afterwards, in the year
415, she herself was seized by the Alexandrian rabble on account
of her paganism, dragged to a church, and torn to pieces.
Synesius does not appear to have lived to learn of her ghastly
end. He may have been dead by 413.

Had Synesius succeeded in achieving his service in the new
Christian community, as he had hoped, 'not as a decline but
as an ascent to the heights of philosophy' (Ep. 11 ad Presb.
[Hercher p. 648]; 96 [95] ad Olymp. [Hercher p. 696])? No
word has survived that would suggest that he repented or was
even troubled in his conscience. As bishop, Synesius knew that
he was in the place to which his God and his native land had
called him and where it was his duty to stay. Like Basil, he
deliberately sacrificed his leisure and philosophy to the demands imposed on him by the common weal. He was more
faithful in this respect than Gregory of Nyssa, who was never
able to overcome the individualistic rhetorician in him.

But one recalls Gregory of Nyssa when one sees how he
secured for himself in the inner realm of his personality a kingdom of his own where he enjoyed more freedom than he showed
to the outside world. How many bishops may there not have
been on the thrones of the Greek Church who were like him?
Classical culture and Platonic philosophy never died out in the
Byzantine Empire, and if Synesius already believed in the possibility of preserving his old convictions even when he had become a Christian and a bishop, the Christianizing of Platonism
and the Platonizing of Christianity became a regular tradition
in the following age. Even where it was impossible to ignore

the differences the Church usually left in peace the philosophers who behaved like Synesius. The real crises and conflicts always began where the theologians tried to take their profession quite seriously and endeavoured to make the peculiar and characteristic quality of the Christian Faith binding on themselves and their Church.

CHAPTER XI

JOHN CHRYSOSTOM

GREEK Christianity knew no conflict between Church and State in the medieval sense. There were struggles for power, but they were always concerned with power inside the Church itself. Even the greatest bishops never demanded to be heard on political questions or to make political decisions. On the contrary, it was the Emperor, as the Christian holder of supreme earthly power, who ordered and supervised the affairs of the Church. Limits were set to his action only in the innermost spiritual and sacerdotal spheres; this did not prevent him from intervening in party disputes and using his authority to decide the issue. The real problem in the East was therefore to get the Emperor on one's own side and, with his help, to disarm one's ecclesiastical enemies. Where that failed, all that remained was the protest of faith, the direct appeal to God's commandment and truth, and the way of martyrdom. The Greek Church never lacked men who were prepared to go that way if necessary.

John Chrysostom was no martyr of the orthodox Faith; questions of dogma played scarcely any part in his life. But he was the prototype of the Churchman who remains loyal to his spiritual mission to the end and who would think it treason to have any regard for political circumstances and the powerful of this world. If it had been possible for him to remain what he essentially was—the indefatigable preacher and interpreter of the word of God, the teacher and true admonisher of his congregation, the friend and helper of all the poor, oppressed, and needy—perhaps his life would have ended peacefully. But the brilliant gifts which he possessed and the love and admiration which his work called forth raised him against his will to the highest position, one of decisive importance in the world of ecclesiastical politics. Here the only man who could hold his own was one who commanded not only the spiritual gifts of the preacher and pastor but also political acumen and tactical skill, which Chrysostom lacked. He was, however, far too conscientious and energetic not to take seriously the duties of leadership and government which his office imposed on him. He thus became involved in problems and conflicts in which he was bound to go under.

The world from which Chrysostom came was different from that of the Fathers we have discussed in the last few chapters. He was born in Antioch, the Syrian metropolis on the Orontes. He was therefore no country gentleman and ruler by descent but a child of the great city and its motley life. The environment in which he was brought up was upper-class and well-to-do. He received the whole of his early education from women, as was the case with so many devout ascetics, since his father, a high-ranking officer, had died young. If we are to take him at his word, he led rather a wild life for a time, 'ensnared by the lusts of the world' (De Sacerd. I, 3). But the examples which he gives—the enjoyment of dainty foods, delight in the theatre, and attendance at public court proceedings—show at once that we need not take these conventional self-accusations too seriously. He spent a well-cared-for youth in the midst of what he calls the 'blazing house' of the life of the great city. At eighteen John underwent baptism, which was in his eyes the seal of a spiritual life, and only three years later, after concluding his general education in rhetoric, he was ordained anagnost, or reader. This might have been the beginning of a religious career, but it was still only a time of preparation in his life. Two forces shaped his further development: the monastic ideal, which had such deep roots in Syria, and the excellent school of Antiochene Biblical scholarship. Chrysostom settled in the neighbourhood of Antioch as an ascetic and devoted himself to spiritual exercises and serious theological work.

Monasticism was already widespread in and around Antioch

at this period. The monks were the saints of the people, who
went on pilgrimage to their caves and cells, and they included
distinguished theologians in their ranks. They quite often sup-
plied the Church with its leading clergy and bishops. Chrysostom devoted himself enthusiastically to the monastic ideals.
The conquest of the base earthly passions, the moral discipline
of a selfless love concentrated on God, seemed to him the real
fulfilment of the Christian commandment. He complied with
the ascetic exercises of fasting, enduring cold, and praying, with
an obstinacy which did lasting injury to his health, and perhaps
he really did at first consider spending his whole life like this
as a monk. On the other hand, he was much too active a character and far too missionary-minded to find lasting satisfaction
in the pursuit of ascetic perfection. The inner peace to which
the monk aspires, to the best of his ability, is not without a
secret egotism (De Compunct. I, 6) and can never be achieved
by physical exertion alone. Another and more noble fire is
needed, the love for Christ which automatically binds us to our
fellow-Christians. It is, moreover, a tremendous error to believe that only the monk is committed to the pursuit of perfection. Christ called all men and made no distinction between the
ascetic and the secular life. Love, the supreme value, is common
to both. Paul has 'required the same love of the people of the
world as Christ required of his disciples' (Adv. Oppugn. 3, 14).
The monk merely finds it easier to attain the goal because he
renounces marriage and a thousand other temptations from the
very outset. Those are to be admired all the more who stand in
the midst of the world as priests, bringing salvation and sanctification to others. Later on, as a young clergyman, Chrysostom
wrote a treatise, On the Priesthood, in which he further developed
these ideas, taking Gregory of Nazianzus as his point of departure. Those who are permitted in fear and trembling to
perform the most holy sacrifice at the altar, who forgive or
retain men's sins, aware that only God in heaven can confirm
their judgment, ascend into truly superhuman spheres. It is not
surprising that a monk may well shrink from this dangerous

office, but it is the greater of the two religious vocations. 'Anyone who compares the torments of the monastic life with a properly conducted spiritual office will find the difference as great as between a private person and the Emperor' (*De Sacerd.* VI, 5). It is clear that the venturesome path from monk to bishop which Basil the Great had decided to tread, with a heavy heart, was beginning to be a solidly built highway open to all.

Even before the beginning of his monastic life, Chrysostom had entered upon his theological studies. The patriarchate of Antioch had had to take a back seat in the disturbances caused by the Arian controversy and give way to Alexandria and also to the young capital of Constantinople, but the first place in which the disciples were called Christians (Acts xi. 26)—a distinction to which Chrysostom draws attention again and again —still proudly claimed to be the centre of theological activities and education. The traditions of serious scholarship which had been developed in Pergamum were revived in the Antiochene school. At this period it possessed in the great Diodorus of Tarsus a leader of outstanding importance and acknowledged sanctity. Diodorus, who had gloriously withstood the oppression of the 'Arians' under the Emperor Valens, was a dialectician trained in the Aristotelian school and a philologist. He was also a dogmatist who gave precise reasons for the doctrine of the two natures of Christ and encouraged his pupils to discuss all imaginable theological problems. But his main influence on Chrysostom was as a Biblical scholar. It was from Diodorus that Chrysostom learned to value and explore the New Testament as the source of all true knowledge and laid the basis of his comprehensive knowledge of the Bible. He did not, it is true, himself become a scholar. Chrysostom never mastered any language but his native Greek and had to rely on experts for his knowledge of the original text of the Old Testament and its Syriac parallels. But he never disowned his careful philological training. He took it seriously and believed that all historical and psychological considerations must serve to establish the original meaning of the text itself and not be used prematurely to find arbitrary theological interpretations and allegorical speculations of one kind and another. Chrysostom also studied the personal characters of and differences between the various authors of the Bible, and on many exegetical problems his wise judgment still carries weight today. Ultimately, however, all scholarly exegesis must subserve the preaching of the gospel, in which alone, by teaching, rousing, and edifying the hearers, it can attain its full effect and development. In the sermon we hear the voice of Christ and the call of his apostles. It should reveal the forgiving love which God has shown by sending his Son and, by the sacrifice on the Cross, arouse our love for him and awaken us to a new life of discipleship and good works. Chrysostom did not contribute to the dogmatic elaboration of Christological theory nor take much interest in the academic disputes of the day in this field. What interested him was the rousing of men's hearts, the kindling of their moral energy, developing in them pure love and an unfeigned spiritual outlook. It was no accident that St. Matthew's was his favourite Gospel, and his love for St. Paul, of whom he wrote a complete exposition, was directed above all to the devotional and moral aspects of the Letters. The heart of the Pauline doctrine of justification meant nothing to Chrysostom. Pelagius referred to him (Chrysostom) as his authority.

It was probably thanks to the old Bishop Meletius, who attached importance to an educated clergy, that Chrysostom returned to the city from his cave in the mountains in the winter of 380–81. Meletius ordained him deacon of his cathedral before his last journey to Constantinople for the Council (see above, p. 111). Later on Chrysostom was also ordained priest. It is said that owing to excessive ascetic exertions at this time he came near to a physical breakdown, so that to live any longer in solitude was in any case out of the question. We find him engaged henceforth as an organizer of charity, as a preacher and pastor entirely devoted to the practical service of the Church. He also continued to devote himself to literary activities which developed out of his day-to-day work and are sober, realistic, and natural. He wrote a treatise of consolation for one mentally ill, another for a young widow, a treatise on the education of children, a warning against second marriages. He also wrote a special treatise against the monastic abuse of co-habitation with consecrated virgins, the so-called *subintroductae* (spiritual marriage). In a series of apologetic lectures he sup-plied the evidence, for Jews and pagans, that Christ was the Son of God. By special request Chrysostom also preached on con-troversial theological problems; but the great mass of his ser-mons were simple interpretations of Biblical texts, not devoted to a particular subject, but homilies in which the text is paraphrased and applied. In this way Chrysostom often thoroughly discussed and preached on whole books of the Bible. The sermons were then published or incorporated in his *Commentaries*. But even in his purely literary work he preferred the form of the homily.

As a preacher he was indefatigable, and he influenced his own world and posterity above all through his sermons. 'I cannot let a day pass without feeding you with the treasures of the Scriptures' (*Hom. in Genes.* 28, 1; 82, 2). He was not given the surname 'Chrysostom' (golden-mouthed) until the sixth cen-tury, but admiration for his preaching was already widespread in his own time. It was not long before he became the most popular speaker in Antioch. Several stenographers used to take down his words, and there was loud applause whenever he spoke, even when he was preaching real sermons, not mere lectures; the charm, freshness, and naturalness of his speech were immediately attractive. In appearance he was plain and homely. His voice was not strong, and he was often in poor health. But preaching was a vital necessity to him. Just as the congregation hungered to listen, so, he said, he hungered to preach. 'Preaching makes me healthy; as soon as I open my mouth, all tiredness is gone' (*Hom. Post Terrae Motum*, Migne 50, 713 f.). Chrysostom spoke a pure, correct Attic, and it was clear that he was a trained orator. But he avoided the usual bombast and ostentation and expressed himself very simply in form as well as in matter. He wanted everyone to be able to understand him. His sermons were usually well-prepared, but he could also digress and take up spontaneous suggestions from his audience without the slightest difficulty. Unaffected contact with his congregation is a mark of the true pastor and was typical of Chrysostom's whole nature. When his sermons were published the personal digressions were usually deleted.

Practical and moral problems were paramount in his interpretation and application of the Biblical texts. His sermons contain a great deal of exhortation and moralizing. He often complained about the lack of moral improvement in his congregation, but he also knew when to encourage and praise them; the supremely important thing was to keep alive in them the delight in goodness. The 'good', however, consists not only in devotional exercises and ascetic training but above all in deeds of love and social service within the Church. How much suffering lurks in a great city; how many cripples and beggars crowd in front of every church door; how many sick there are whose sufferings cry to heaven! Chrysostom gives deeply affecting descriptions of the sufferings of the sick who lie on straw and dung with their ulcers and deformities, who have no clothes to cover them, who freeze and starve. Not everything should be left to the Church and its relief workers. People should themselves go to the baths, to the almshouses and hospitals which the Church maintains, and give a helping hand. The lurid contrast between rich and poor, the senseless luxury on the one hand and the extreme poverty on the other within the one society which calls itself Christian, is a further favourite topic on which Chrysostom dwells with relentless candour. The rich man and poor Lazarus, the sufferings of Job, the injunctions of the Sermon on the Mount, the example of the apostolic Church are biblical examples to which he returns again and again. One of his frequent subjects of complaint is the congregation's insatiable lust for pleasure. The old mania for circuses and the theatre, 'this universal school of dissolution', this 'training-ground of unchastity' and 'throne of pestilence' (*Hom. 6, 1 de Poen.*) are, he complains, still rampant. At the popular festivals in the city part of Daphne there have been desperately few changes since the evil days of paganism. On such days even the churches are empty and the preacher is made to feel his complete powerlessness.

In times of trouble or when disaster threatens, the atmosphere changes just as rapidly and everyone crowds into church for spiritual help. Thus it was in the spring of the year 387 when Chrysostom delivered the famous series of sermons 'On the Statues'. Owing to an increase in taxation the people had, in a sudden tumult, defaced the statues of the Emperor and terrible punishment was expected. The whole city, in which individual executions had already taken place, was paralysed with fear and looked like 'a forsaken beehive' (*Hom. de Stat.* 2, 1). Chrysostom visited the prisoners, went personally to the commander, and tried to comfort the people and prepare them for any eventuality. He emphasized that the immediate responsibility for the disaster lay not with the old, established citizens but with the foreign rabble; but the manifold sins of the people, above all, their swearing and blaspheming, had made them all partly to blame. It was now becoming clear what all the wealth and glory of the world were really worth in time of danger. They must put their whole trust in God and not set the pagans a bad example by cowardice and despondency. The Bishop of Antioch then travelled to Constantinople, and after anxious weeks of waiting the city was granted the imperial pardon mainly thanks to the intercession of monks and clergy.

In the year 397 an important event occurred: the death of the metropolitan Bishop Nectarius of Constantinople. As a layman and praetor he had been promoted to this position by Theodosius at the Council of 381, since the elected bishop, Gregory of Nazianzus, had been unable to ride the storm of the conflicting ecclesiastical groups. The unworthy competition for the succession was now renewed. Candidates and interested parties made their voices heard on every side. In particular, the Patriarch of Alexandria, Theophilus, embarked at once on his usual efforts to secure the influential post for someone agreeable and submissive to himself. The less gifted Emperor Arcadius was utterly unlike his father Theodosius and proved quite helpless, but his all-powerful favourite Eutropius decided to take the matter into his own hands. Without disclosing anything to the various representatives of the Church, he tried to prevent the threatening confusion in the same way as in the year 381, by promoting a man who stood outside the turmoil of ecclesiastical politics, except that this time it was not a layman but a theologian of high standing, capable of satisfying the demands of ecclesiastical decorum and representing the Church at court and in the capital. Chrysostom was already famous as a preacher and writer far beyond the confines of his native city. But care was taken not to drop the slightest hint of the appointment, even to Chrysostom himself, to avoid arousing any opposition in Antioch. One day he merely received an order from the highest official, the Comes Orientis, who resided in the city, instructing him to appear in a small martyrs' chapel outside the gates, for a discussion. A coach awaited him there which he was forced to board, and he was taken post-haste to Constantinople. There the unsuspecting bishops were already assembled for the election, and Theophilus himself was forced, after vain protests, to consecrate Chrysostom. Overnight the powerless little priest of Antioch had become the leading bishop of the East, the spiritual ruler of Constantinople, the preacher whose duty it was to preach before the Emperor and his brilliant court.

Needless to say, Chrysostom had never desired such a turn of events and was not in the least prepared for it. But once appointed, he did not hesitate to tackle the new tasks which confronted him with remarkable vigour. No less than before did he regard preaching and pastoral work as his foremost tasks, and in this respect he fulfilled all the hopes that had been placed in him. His services were the best attended in Constantinople, and soon a large circle of personal followers and admirers gathered around him, especially from the world of devout ladies who supported him in his spiritual efforts and put large funds at his disposal. Chrysostom tried to reorganize and expand the social relief work and nursing activities. With this end in view he restricted the building of new churches and submitted the whole administration and system of accountancy to a thorough scrutiny. He was not at all satisfied with conditions among the clergy. In Constantinople the system of 'spiritual marriages' had spread to the parochial clergy, and various unworthy priests had to be deprived of their office. Monastic vagabonds were banished to monasteries and confined to a strictly religious life. Chrysostom also took up the struggle against heretics; he refused to tolerate their conventicles any longer. For all his personal gentleness and readiness to discuss, he was by no means 'liberal' in this regard and believed in the rights of the Catholic State Church. 'The Jews and pagans must learn that the Christians are the saviours, protectors, directors, and teachers of the city' (*Hom. de Stat.* 1, 12). Even the special political needs of his diocese found in him a clear-sighted champion who vigorously trod new paths. The Council that took place in 381 had made the Bishop of New Rome next in rank to the Western Bishop of Old Rome, but his relationship to the neighbouring metropolitans still needed to be clarified—in fact, all he really possessed was an isolated city without a hinterland of any importance. Under Chrysostom the importance of the patriarchate of Constantinople grew. What he had in mind was the position occupied by Antioch in Syria. Among other things, he deposed the unworthy Bishop of Ephesus, intervened in other seriously neglected dioceses in Asia Minor, and created order. The five years of uninterrupted activity which were granted to him as bishop laid the foundations for the later development of Constantinople.

Opposition to his policy, and to the whole spirit of reform which he introduced, was inevitable. Hitherto the people had been accustomed to expect the bishop of the capital city to live in magnificent state and appear as representative of the Church on public occasions. He was expected to play a part in the social life of the court and keep open house and table for all ecclesiastical visitors to the capital. Chrysostom reduced his entertaining to the barest minimum. He ate alone, introduced the strictest economies, and never tired of stressing that he considered care for the poor and activity in the spiritual and ascetic spheres the essential tasks of his office. He rejected the previous spirit of live and let live at the expense of the Church. He soon made enemies of a number of bishops who were always pottering about the capital and the court instead of looking after their own churches at home. His constant attacks on public amusements and the luxury of the upper classes annoyed many influential people in the city. They came thoroughly to disapprove of this choleric ascetic. Occasions for enmity and intrigue were never lacking in Constantinople. Chrysostom took the noble but dangerous course of ignoring these things and keeping steadfastly to the direction he had set himself. In these circumstances the support which he had and was able to maintain at the court was all-important.

To begin with, he had been received with great kindness and good will. Arcadius, who was regarded as exceptionally devout, received the new patriarch, whose reputation for sanctity had preceded him, with great warmth and joy. But he had little influence on the decisions of the government. It was much more important for the new bishop to establish good relations with the lively and enterprising Empress Eudoxia. She, too, welcomed the new patriarch with high hopes. At one of the first religious ceremonies which he organized, the solemn entry of the relics of Phocas, Bishop of Sinope in Pontus, she condescended to carry the martyr's remains through the city in a procession which took place at night. In the sermon which followed the ceremony the bishop did not fail to draw attention to this admirable expression of supreme devotion on the part of the Empress. When the need arose, Chrysostom could command the extravagant style of courtly rhetoric, and he did not spare himself in praise for the pious devotion to Christ of the imperial house. It is evident that in the early years his position at court was not at all bad. When Eutropius was overthrown in the year 399, it was the intercession of Chrysostom that saved him. Eutropius fled to the altar in the cathedral. Once again Chrysostom took the opportunity of pointing out to the congregation the frailty of all earthly greatness, and he mercilessly reproached the miserable man with a list of his sins. But he was able to save his life. Ill-feeling against Chrysostom began among some of the gay ladies-in-waiting and seems then to have clouded his relationship with Eudoxia. Hostile tale-bearers did not fail to misinterpret and falsify certain innocent remarks which he made in his sermons. In particular, he is said to have harmed himself by taking an interest in a widow who had been wrongly deprived of her possessions by Eudoxia, and in this connection it is possible that he really did compare her with the Old Testament Queen Jezebel (I Kings xxi). All these things led to disaster, however, only when his enemies in the hierarchy were able to join forces with the court and so outmanoeuvre him.

The jealousy of the Alexandrian patriarch toward Constantinople was of long standing and was constantly receiving fresh nourishment from Chrysostom's activities. The hostility came to a head when an action was brought against Theophilus in Constantinople by a large group of monks, led by the four so-called 'Tall Brothers', who wanted to lodge a complaint against the high-handed rule of the patriarch and the injustices that had been done to them. Theophilus had branded them off-hand as malignant heretics because of their Origenist training, and he had finally banished them from Egypt. Pursued by his spiteful circular letters, they now appealed to Chrysostom for help. Chrysostom was by no means blind to the dangers of the situation and tried to calm and put the brake on the angry men, whom he lodged outside the official church hostel. He wrote a polite and correct letter to his Alexandrian colleague and did all he could to prevent the conflict from spreading. But Theophilus refused to negotiate, and the monks got in touch with the government, which accepted their writ and called a Council to settle the matter, at which Theophilus was to appear as defendant and Chrysostom was to sit in judgment. His embittered and aggressive colleague was thus unwillingly pushed to extremes, and the situation moved on to a final catastrophe.

Theophilus did not consider appearing straight away, but he fully grasped the situation and wasted no time in dealing with it. He had inquiries made in Antioch about his rival's early life, but they failed to reveal anything to his discredit. He urged on a narrow-minded enemy of the heretics, Bishop Epiphanius of Salamis, to go to Constantinople and propagandize against Chrysostom. He got in touch with the bishops who had been reprimanded by Chrysostom and spared no money to encourage the anti-Chrysostom party at court. The dissemination of more or less forged sermon notes containing personal attacks on the Empress and the luxury of her life at court proved to be particularly effective. When Theophilus finally arrived in Constantinople he brought with him, against express instructions, a whole host of Egyptian bishops and made a pompous entry into the city escorted by this entourage. He took up residence in a palace belonging to Eudoxia. He turned down an invitation from Chrysostom. He did all he could to exchange the role of the accused for that of the accuser. In spite of the menacing omens, Chrysostom took no action for the moment. This was correct enough but undoubtedly the most stupid thing he could have done. Indeed, when Arcadius, who evidently still supported him, finally gave orders for the hearing to begin, Chrysostom declared himself incompetent to preside, out of exaggerated respect for legal propriety and perhaps also in the hope of propitiating and assuaging Theophilus. But he thereby only made it all the easier for Theophilus to take further arbitrary action.

In September of the year 403 Theophilus held a synod of his supporters outside the city gates in a monastery by an oak tree, and summoned Chrysostom to appear before them. Needless to say, Chrysostom refused to appear, but he did not merely protest and leave it at that. With an excess of humility and conscientiousness he declared himself ready to appear provided his proven enemies were removed from the group that purposed to pass judgment on him. A further delegation which Chrysostom sent to the 'Synod of the Oak' was soundly flogged, and proceedings against him were opened in his absence. A decision was reached in the shortest possible time. We need not quote all the forty-six points of the indictment. The complaints about the extension of his sphere of influence were specially significant. But generally speaking, it was all a frantic mixture of libel, childish or deliberate misunderstanding, and political accusation, the purpose of which was clear from the start—to prove Chrysostom guilty of bribery and corruption: 'he eats on his own and lives like Cyclops; he has committed acts of violence and insulted the Imperial Majesty'. The judgment was nevertheless confirmed by the weak Emperor. The people were exasperated, and if Chrysostom had wished he could probably have resisted. But he was not the man to exploit opportunities for revolution, let alone organize resistance on his own initiative. Calmly and quietly he gave himself up to the soldiers and allowed himself to be taken from the city in the dead of night. It seemed as if his role as Bishop of Constantinople were over.

Suddenly, however, the tide turned. The haphazardness and capriciousness of the Imperial Church administration become all too obvious when we learn the reason why the alleged criminal was recalled, only a day after his banishment. Eudoxia, who had clearly been pulling wires behind the scenes during this whole episode, had a miscarriage. In her horror, she believed that it was a judgment from heaven and gave orders for Chrysostom to return at once. He had trouble in securing a more or less legal annulment of the sentence passed against him. Everything was to be forgiven and forgotten. But once disturbed, it was not easy to restore the relationship. Only a few weeks later the tension had reached menacing proportions again and disaster loomed ahead. During the dedication of a statue in honour of the Empress the noise of the popular rejoicings had upset divine worship. The irritated comments

11

about the disturbance which escaped from Chrysostom naturally reached the ears of Eudoxia. Then, on the festival of John
the Baptist, he began his sermon with a reference to Herodias,
who was demanding the head of the Baptist 'once again', and
his enemies were probably justified in interpreting this as another hostile allusion to the Empress. The old opposition was
not dead. It is true that Theophilus had decamped, but the
court's episcopal advisers now took the position that the proceedings against Chrysostom had never been concluded.
Eudoxia took the matter up and declared that she would not
attend the cathedral again until the case had been concluded and
the bishop cleared of the charges preferred against him. In fact,
it was scarcely possible to carry out this proposal. The intention
was obviously to get rid of Chrysostom without further re-
course to violence, and he again proved quite helpless in the face
of the intrigues which were set in motion against him from all
sides. On the one hand, he resolutely refused voluntarily to
leave the flock with which God had entrusted him. On the
other hand, he did nothing to prevent a new and completely
unauthorized assembly from conspiring against him. When the
situation was still not cleared up by Easter in the year 404, the
government tried to prevent by force of arms the baptisms
which were normally conducted by the bishop at this season,
and their action led to bloodshed. In the end, the unwilling
Emperor was forced once again to sign a decree of banishment.
Chrysostom called together his faithful clergy and bishops for
a final prayer in the sacristy and exhorted the faithful deacon-
esses and female assistants not to grow cold in spiritual zeal. He
then took the necessary measures to prevent disturbances, and
for the second time he went quite calmly into exile and cap-
tivity with a military escort.

A confused situation that had become quite intolerable had
thereby been brought to an end. It is clear that Arcadius's in-
dolence and susceptibility to outside influences were mainly
responsible. He had been incapable of taking any vigorous
action, leaving all decisions to his wife and the partisan clerical

advisers who crowded around her. Chrysostom himself had scorned to enter the fluctuating ground on which alone the battle might have been won. He was bound to be defeated in the end, although fate had twice appeared to offer him a chance of victory. He was to complete the way that still lay ahead of him not as a prince and ruler of the Church but as a martyr to his office and his Faith.

By banishing Chrysostom the Emperor had probably merely wanted to terminate a desperate situation, with no desire to hurt either him or his followers. But his enemies saw to it that this was not the end of the matter. Immediately after his departure, Chrysostom's cathedral went up in flames for reasons which were never explained, and, needless to say, his followers were made responsible. For their part, some of his supporters refused to have anything to do with the new bishop, and they were cruelly persecuted. The treatment and reception which Chrysostom received on his long journey also varied according to the attitude of his brethren of the Church. The numerous letters which he wrote to his old friends give a vivid account of his situation and his feelings. Letter-writing was considered an art at this period, and these letters therefore still retain a slightly self-conscious air which no educated Greek of the post-classical age ever completely lost. Above all, however, they move us by the humanity and purity of thought which they reveal. Chrysostom felt very weak and did not deny that he sometimes suffered greatly from bad treatment, lack of sleep, cold, lack of medicines, and so on; but again and again he tries to comfort his correspondent with the assurance that he is feeling better. He tries to encourage and console his friends, and even from a distance he remains their pastor.

When he arrived at his destination, inhospitable Cucusus in Lower Armenia, his situation began to improve a little. His greatest grief was that he hardly ever had a chance to preach. But his friends saw to it that he did not lack money, with which, once again, he tried to help others. His friends kept him supplied with news and informed him of all the efforts that were

being made on his behalf. Chrysostom took an interest in everything, and gave warnings and advice. Letters were his greatest
joy; nothing worried him more than when they failed to arrive,
and when his former friends no longer wrote to him owing to
their laziness or fear. But his thoughts were by no means concentrated entirely on Constantinople and his followers, his
clergy, and his poor. He sought out new tasks for the Church.
He had formerly concerned himself with the conversion and
care of the Goths who lived in Constantinople. He now turned
his attention to nearby Persia and pondered on the possibility
of a thorough-going Christian mission in that country—a problem to which hardly any other leader of the Greek Church had
given any thought. He also tried to keep in touch with the
Bishop of Rome and other influential representatives of the
Western and Eastern Churches. He did not abandon his cause,
and he continued to hope for peace in the Church and the
victory of the right.

The fact that these efforts were not a complete failure probably contributed to his ultimate destruction. Only a year later,
in the late summer of 405, he was forced to leave Cucusus,
which was threatened by barbarians. He came to Arabissus, and
here too he was followed by a stream of pilgrims who wanted
to see, visit, and speak to him. In the high summer of 407
instructions arrived to move him to the farthest corner of the
Empire: to Pityus, on the Black Sea. According to his own
admission, nothing tired him out so much as travelling, and it
was evidently intended to kill him by making him trudge
through the roughest tracts of country. He was refused any relief. The seriously ailing man was exposed to the heat of the sun
and the driving rain; he was given no chance to rest; he was
driven on relentlessly. Even on the eve of his death he was
forced to march, with a high fever, five miles to the town of
Comana. There he was lovingly received by the little congregation, but he had to travel on the very next morning. After
nearly three and a half miles of walking, he collapsed completely. He was taken back to Comana, wrapped in a white

shroud, and given the holy sacrament for the last time. Chrysostom crossed himself and died with a word of praise for his whole life: 'Glory be to God for everything! Amen.'

The struggle around his name and right continued. The Western world refused as obstinately as ever to recognize the validity of his deposal and banishment, and in the Greek world too it became increasingly difficult to hush up the obvious injustice that had been done. In the year 438 the son of Arcadius, the Emperor Theodosius II, had the saint's remains solemnly interred in the Apostolic Church of Constantinople. Chrysostom's posthumous fame was immense. The writings of no other Father of the Church were read so much or disseminated in such a wealth of manuscripts. He was translated early into Latin and various Oriental languages. Even today John Chrysostom enjoys the love and veneration of all denominations. He whose life was embittered and destroyed by his enemies now has no enemies at all. As a theologian he was neither profound nor original. He was a typical representative of his school, of his period and its ecclesiastical and ascetic ideals. One can, however, get an impression from him of the moral and spiritual forces which were still alive in the worldly State Church in spite of the many disappointing bishops who brought it no honour.

His sermons show that theology was still able to fulfil its task in the Church to a very large extent. The homilies of Chrysostom are probably the only ones from the whole of Greek antiquity which at least in part are still readable today as Christian sermons. They reflect something of the authentic life of the New Testament, just because they are so ethical, so simple, and so clear-headed.

CHAPTER XII

CYRIL OF ALEXANDRIA

THE struggle between Chrysostom and Theophilus was not merely a conflict between two personalities: two regions, two theological traditions, and two fundamentally different intellectual and spiritual attitudes were competing against one another. In Chrysostom the Greek legacy had become wholly ethical, ascetic, and saintly, and so deeply permeated by the spirit of Christianity that it was unconquerable and triumphed even in his death. But it must not be overlooked that his opponent, the Patriarch of Alexandria, was, at any rate to begin with, the political victor. Egypt, which at this period was not accounted part of the Greek 'East', was ecclesiastically an extremely centralized world of its own, and the tradition of imperious orthodoxy embodied in its 'Popes' (it was here that the word first acquired its official connotation) had never been checked. It extended from Demetrius, by way of Athanasius, to Theophilus and in the following generation was to be incorporated once again in a powerful figure who was not inferior to his predecessors in consistency of effort and surpassed them in the audacity of his intentions. This was Bishop Cyril, the last great Father of the Church, and the most distinguished saint of Byzantine orthodoxy. As a moral character he is more than open to attack. 'I do not believe', said Cardinal Newman, still somewhat ashamed, 'that Cyril would have agreed that his outward acts should be taken as the measure of his inner sanctity.' But Cyril dug the bed through which the stream of dogmatic developments has subsequently passed so deeply that, generally speaking, it has never left it since. With him, whom even the West extols as *doctor ecclesiae*, we may conclude our series of studies of Greek Fathers of the Church.

The typical marks of an Egyptian hierarch were stamped so intensely on Cyril's personality that it hardly seems to matter that we know almost nothing about his youth and early development. He was a scion of the same great Alexandrian family to which his uncle and predecessor Theophilus had belonged. He was probably destined for a career in the Church from an early age. At any rate, he took part in the Synod of the Oak in the year 403, as a member of his uncle's entourage. For the rest of his life Theophilus regarded the removal of Chrysostom from his throne, which resulted from that Synod, as a justified triumph of his Church. The memory of this event determined Cyril's career in the same way as Athanasius had been influenced by his participation in the Council of Nicaea. After the death of Theophilus there was only a brief electoral campaign. The candidate of the highest rank, the Archdeacon Timotheus, had to give way and Cyril was consecrated, on October 17, 412, only two days after the see had become vacant. He cannot have been very old at the time; he occupied the throne of St. Mark for no less than thirty-two years and he carried out his duties with vigilance and unbroken vigour to the end.

It would be wrong, however, to think of Cyril merely as an ecclesiastical politician and spiritual ruler. Far more than his uncle, he wanted to be a theologian, to represent and personify the true tradition of the Faith as a teacher as well as a bishop. Cyril was a preacher and at the same time an uncommonly prolific writer whose surviving works comprise today ten imposing volumes. Literary work gave him pleasure, and the extent of what he produced testifies to inflexible diligence. As a writer he was not without ambition, although his occasional attempts to attain rhetorical effects and elegance of form fall short of their purpose. His strident style is flat, monotonous, and pompous. He goes straight to the goal he is trying to reach with ponderous forcefulness, but he always succeeds in expressing quite unmistakably what he is trying to say. His books show that he had a clear and methodical mind, although he lacked the refinements which result from careful training. He introduced philosophical concepts only occasionally and quite superficially. He despised the pagan philosophers, who so often 'contradicted' one another and, in Cyril's opinion, stole their best things from Moses. Similarly he regarded Origen as a heretic who had been justly condemned 'because he did not think as a Christian but followed the chatter of the Hellenes' (*Ep. 81*, Migne 77, 373). From Chrysostom he was, not surprisingly, unable and unwilling to learn anything. Under protest, and only when it had become quite unavoidable, did he condescend to restore his name in the diptychs, or official lists of bishops. In his exegesis Cyril keeps to the 'historical' meaning of Scripture, as opposed to the disintegrating spiritualistic interpretation of Origen. But in fact his exegesis was entirely derived from traditional allegory and typology and is hardly concerned at all with the direct, human meaning of the Bible story. His main interest is exclusively dogmatic and polemical. He uses the Bible to refute the false doctrines of the heretics, to establish the true conception of the Trinity and the divine-human person of the Saviour, on which true piety is based. Christian sanctity is consummated in the adoration of these divine mysteries, in the reception of the life-giving sacraments, and in the ascetic virtues of the monastic way of life.

In his understanding of the message of salvation Cyril thinks of himself as the heir of all previous ecclesiastical teachers, above all of the great orthodox luminaries of his own city of Alexandria. Athanasius he considers the spokesman of the Church par excellence. One-third of Cyril's first work on dogmatics, the tremendous *Thesaurus*, or treasury of a true knowledge of the holy and consubstantial Trinity, consists of nothing but an excerpt from the corresponding *Orations* of Athanasius. Moreover, Didymus, a blind theologian of the second half of the fourth century, while he was never mentioned explicitly, since he was a layman and an Origenist, was no less industriously exploited, and through him something of the work of the Cappadocians flowed into Cyril's writings. For the rest, he does not concern himself much with recent theological controversies. His tireless attacks are aimed at the old traditional enemies: Arius, Eunomius, and the 'godless' Emperor Julian, to refute whom he wrote a gigantic work consisting of thirty books. He always presents orthodox doctrines as if they were solid, revealed, traditional facts which only diabolical malice could possibly distort and misinterpret. Christ, as the divine Logos, i.e. as God himself, stands in the centre. As a mere man he would have been no use to mankind. The real purpose of his Incarnation is to unite our nature with the Godhead and to lead it wholly into the divine—just as the elements of the Holy Communion must be filled with divine energy, if they are to convey to us salvation and the life force of eternity. To consider Jesus 'separately' as a mere man therefore seems an utterly godless proceeding. It is the one incarnate Son of God who effects our salvation. Cyril does not regard as serious the danger that the humanity of Jesus may be evaporated or curtailed. It is true that he knows from the condemnation of Apollinaris of Laodicea that the human soul of the Redeemer's person must not be denied; but he is not clear about the theological implications of this. When, in the struggles with his Antiochene enemies, Cyril was later compelled to develop his Christology in greater detail, he did not hesitate to use the Apollinarian formulas, which he wrongly considered Athanasian, and he spoke of the 'one incarnate nature of the God-Logos'. In the light of later dogmatic formulations his Christology was quite inaccurate and Monophysite. But Cyril never doubted that belief in Christ could be rightly professed and defended only in the way to which he was accustomed. He abhorred all 'tolerant' dilutions and discussions of the truth, and where he had power he was always ready to use it mercilessly to suppress all opposition to his spiritual dominion.

The outlook in Egypt at the beginning of his régime was stormy. The bestial murder of Hypatia was organized by the clergy and was laid at any rate indirectly to Cyril's charge. He gave orders for the churches of the Novatians to be closed by force, though hitherto they had enjoyed official toleration as orthodox, morally austere sectarians. There followed expulsions of Jews and heretics, and when the imperial governor tried to intercede for them Cyril fought him too. He would never give way. His spiritual authority was as unassailable in Egypt as was his economic power as lord of the corn fleets and the estates of the Coptic interior. The monks whom he visited, kept posted with circular letters, and tried to shackle to himself, formed his strongest spiritual army. Cyril attempted to terminate his predecessor's struggle against Origenism and the Origenist-trained monks, relying primarily on the uneducated Coptic saints. But even he had to condemn the barbaric crudeness of the so-called 'Anthropomorphites', who conceived God himself in the bodily likeness of a man.

But here again despair gave rise to opposition which refused to go down without a fight. In the year 428 a deputation of Egyptian monks appeared in Constantinople to protest to the Patriarch Nestorius against the violent rule of their spiritual overlord. Cyril described them as a pack of bankrupt failures from the 'muck-heap of Alexandria' (*Ep. 10, ACO* I, 1, p. 111, 22). The internal conflict thus spread to the realm of universal ecclesiastical politics, and a catastrophic development had begun the consequences of which were as yet unforeseeable.

It appears that Cyril immediately realized the gravity of the situation. The resemblance to the Chrysostom affair was obvious and was to some extent generally noticed. After a long period of political weakness an Antiochene monk of high intellectual standing again sat on the throne in the capital city, theologically and morally stern and fearless, but, like Chrysostom, hardly equal to the political intricacies of his task. Once again the Patriarch of Alexandria was arraigned before him by his own subordinates. If Nestorius refused to yield of his own accord Cyril was faced with the question whether he would turn the tables and go over to the attack himself and wind up the old struggle for power with Constantinople and secure his own predominance in the East.

Like his predecessor, Cyril maintained a permanent legation in Constantinople. His 'apocrisiaries' were there in order to conduct negotiations with the Emperor and the patriarch, and we still have some of the letters containing the detailed instructions which they received from Alexandria. When Nestorius informed them, in a perfectly correct manner, about the complaints that had been received, they met him at once with challenging insolence. They declared that it was improper to accept any complaints against such a great bishop, their Pope, at all, especially as he had hitherto recognized Nestorius without the slightest reservation and treated him kindly. When Nestorius stood firm, they hinted that it might be dangerous for him if they were to report back to Alexandria. Nestorius answered proudly that he was not in need of the kind of friendship that obliged him to approve or tolerate the wrong. It appears that Cyril had every reason to prevent a thorough investigation of the affair which was in suspense; but this meant departing from the formally correct method of procedure which had so far been followed. The best way seemed to be to adopt tactics successfully used earlier by Athanasius and to transfer the legal dispute to the plane of religious belief. If the man who criticized Cyril's dubious official acts could be brought under suspicion of a secret heresy, this would divert attention from any previous complaints and the troublesome attacker would become the defendant and his proceedings would lead to his own ruin.

It was not difficult to find reasons for a theological charge, and it may be assumed that Cyril did not have to act against his convictions. Nestorius was a typical representative of Antiochene theology and the sharp distinction which it made between the human and the divine nature of Christ, which was an abomination to Cyril. Unlike Chrysostom, Nestorius, with his intense confidence in himself as a dogmatist, felt called upon to elaborate the doctrine and to secure universal recognition for it. He too had already made a name for himself as an enemy of heretics and sectarians in an around Constantinople. His enemies were only too ready to co-operate with Cyril and to put at his disposal incriminating sermon notes and the like. Ill-feeling had been aroused in particular by the fact that Nestorius had publicly criticized the current description of Mary as 'God-bearer' (*Theotokos*). It is true that, as a fair-minded pastor, he had actually admitted that this term could in a certain sense be used quite devoutly and orthodoxly. But fundamentally it was important to realize that the divine nature as such could neither be born nor become a human being nor suffer and die on the Cross. All these statements must refer to the human aspect of the person of Christ, and Mary had therefore born the man Jesus, not the eternal Logos of God. Nestorius recommended, in order to bring this dangerous dispute to an end, calling her rather 'Mother of Christ' (*Christotokos*), which would satisfy everyone. This was quite consistent with the Antiochene view, but the public refused to be fobbed off with such dry, rational-istic distinctions. The alleged criticism of the dignity and glory of the Mother of God touched a sensitive spot in popular de-votion, and Cyril knew what he was doing when he declared this term 'God-bearer' to be the distinguishing mark of all true faith in Christ. From his theological point of view this was not only quite consistent but it thereby assured him of a widespread response from the masses and their support for his further pro-ceedings. From a historical standpoint the victory which he was to gain over Nestorius must be regarded as the first great triumph of the popular worship of Mary.

It was some time before the conflict was fully developed. As was only to be expected. Nestorius, in his irritation and injured pride, showed little diplomatic skill. He wanted to avoid a break, but he exposed himself by various tactical mistakes, in his confidence that he must act properly and remain in the right. Leaving aside all moral judgments for the moment, it must be admitted that Cyril's adroitness and genius were dis-played in a brilliant light. He gave his assent to every method of silent intrigue and propaganda as well as the usual method of large-scale bribery, in the form of promises and costly 'presents'. While his clumsy, morally austere colleague scoffed at the 'golden arrows' (*ACO* I, 5, p. 43, 17) with which he was to be injured, Cyril indefatigably gathered together the 'material' which was to compromise him, got in touch with every group hostile to Nestorius, and, without making any open attack, fomented the increasing popular hatred for the alleged new heresy. He was not greatly concerned with the truth; outwardly, however, he continued to play the part of the anxious, thoughtful leader who refuses to take action for reasons of purely personal spite, leaving the first steps to his friends and go-betweens.

Two courts of appeal were especially important in the impending conflict: the Emperor in Constantinople and Bishop Celestine of Rome. As a Westerner, Celestine I stood to some extent outside the theological controversy and was, as Nestorius quite right said, 'much too simple to be able to penetrate into the finer meaning of doctrinal truths' (*ACO* I, 4, p. 25, 34). But care was taken to see that Nestorius's Christological theses were laid before him in such a grossly caricatured form that he was at once persuaded to take a stand against these 'obvious blasphemies' (*ACO* I, 2, p. 8, 1). The whole dispute arose because certain dogmas were pushed to logical extremes. Nestorius would later never admit as his opinion the assumption of 'two sons of God' of which he was accused. But his letter to Rome, written in a quiet, friendly tone, omitted to include the usual terms of flattery, while Cyril addressed his younger colleague right away as his 'most holy Father, most beloved of God' and put himself at his disposal with the most diligent humility. He soon had the Pope entirely on his side. In a graciously written letter Celestine appointed him his deputy and instructed him to pursue the dangerous dispute with unremitting energy.

Cyril was less fortunate in Constantinople. He attempted to incite against Nestorius not only the Emperor but also the Empress and above all the energetic Princess Pulcheria. But for the present Theodosius II was still convinced that his patriarch was in the right, and Cyril was suspected of trying to sow dissension in the Emperor's family by dedicating certain theological treatises to different members of the family. Nevertheless, all was not lost at court. Theodosius was a weakling, like his father, and in the habit of giving way to his eunuchs and other unreliable advisers, who were not beyond the reach of Cyril's letters and his gold. An initial success was marked by the fact that to begin with only the religious dispute was assigned to the Council that was summoned to Ephesus at Whitsun, 431, and further proceedings against individual members were expressly forbidden.

Cyril had not waited for the Council to be called. After apparently hesitating for a long time, he now realized that only ruthless speed could assure him of victory. Relying on the unconditional support of Rome, he convened a council of his Egyptian suffragans in Alexandria which forthwith condemned Nestorius as a heretic. The 'anathemas' with which the judgment was supported were based so blatantly and one-sidedly on the complete unity of the person of Christ in the divine Logos, that they were rightly interpreted as Apollinarian by the Antiochenes and entirely rejected. But the partisan and precipitate *fait accompli* gave Cyril the chance of treating Nestorius in Ephesus as a notorious heretic with whom fellowship or negotiation of any kind was out of the question. The local Bishop of Ephesus, who was striving for his own independence, had been persuaded to join the anti-Constantinople party and put all the churches in the city at Cyril's disposal. Nestorius was virtually excluded. In spite of the protests of the imperial official charged with the administration of the Council, the Council gave up waiting for the missing Syrians and the Roman legates, and Cyril's followers were recognized as the legally constituted synod. The Council did not hesitate formally to excommunicate Nestorius as a heretic. The jubilant populace celebrated in the streets the fall of the 'enemy of the Holy Virgin' and the honour of the 'great, sublime, and glorious Mother of God'.

When Bishop John of Antioch and Nestorius's other supporters finally arrived, all they could do was to hold a separate synod which condemned Cyril and his followers. To begin with, the helpless Emperor recognized the truth of both parties' views and had both Cyril and Nestorius taken in custody. Protracted and complicated negotiations began in which Cyril, with his 'well-known methods of persuasion', namely bribery (*ACO* I, 1, 5, p. 136, 17), quickly won some points. But the decisive thing was that Nestorius was the first to give in and offered his resignation, thinking that he must serve the cause of peace. His resignation was accepted, and he was allowed to retire to his old Antiochene monastery. Cyril was also allowed to escape to Alexandria, where he at once proclaimed on every side the triumph of truth and victory over his godless opponents, as the result of the sacred synod. With this completely untrue assertion he finally prevailed, but only several decades later.

The illegal sessions which he had organized with his followers are still described as the 'Third General Council of Ephesus', which honoured the Mother of God and saved the true Faith in Christ from misrepresentation and distortion. And, as a result of the Council, Cyril himself was canonized.

Did Cyril ever really believe his own account of events? Probably that is the wrong way to put the question. It presupposes a love of justice and an impartiality of which the passionate and embittered hierarch was never capable. Dogmatic, violent, and cunning, full of the greatness of his seat and the dignity of his office, he never considered anything as right unless it was useful to him in the furtherance of his power and authority and accorded with his theological tradition and training. The brutality and unscrupulousness of his methods never worried him, and the fact that similar methods were still more often used in later theological conflicts may be pleaded in extenuation. The most serious charge against him is that in the end he was not even true to his theological principles, but for tactical reasons, in order to conserve his outward victories, he really surrendered most of the points he had maintained in Alexandria and Ephesus. After the abdication of Nestorius and Cyril's escape from Ephesus the opposition party had not given up the theological struggle. On the contrary, under the skilful leadership of John of Antioch, a storm of protest was raised throughout the East against the cynical condemnation of a Christological conception to which the majority of Greek-trained theologians and bishops still adhered. The government supported the protest, and in the end Cyril had to give way. After protracted and extremely disagreeable negotiations he accepted a compromise formula in 433 which simply ignored his most outstanding theses and which Nestorius would have accepted at any time. But this was precisely the point on which Cyril remained inexorable: the case of Nestorius was never reopened. He remained condemned as a heretic, and to the outside world Cyril was still 'the man who had unmasked the blasphemers and led the truth to victory'. Indeed, he did not rest until the unhappy man who had been abandoned by his own friends and supporters was wrenched from his Antiochene refuge and deported to Cyril's own territory. He was interned in a remote spot on the edge of the Egyptian Desert; he survived Cyril and died fifteen years later, inwardly unbroken to the end.

One is inclined to deny the theological significance of Cyril altogether in view of his abominable behaviour, and to see in him merely the coldly calculating power politician who sacrificed everything on the altar of his personal success. We have already said that such an interpretation is not in accordance with Cyril's own feeling. It is not enough to see in this subordination of serious theological interests to purely political considerations merely the expression of partisan subjectivism and passion. It was rather the expression of a particular sort of Churchmanship which was no longer tied to theology and tried to maintain the victory of the Faith by enforcing the acceptance of ecclesiastical authority and the 'true' ecclesiastical tradition.

The old problem of the frontiers of theology, which Athanasius had already sensed and Basil had pondered theologically, is now solved in a way which justifies the corruption of systematic thought and theological conscientiousness. After all, the herd thinks in accordance with the teacher's wishes (*ACO* I, 4, p. 227, 19). The important thing is no longer the clarity and purity of the formulas obtained, so long as the right men, the men of the right party, are in power to enforce them. The peace of the Church which has been won by tactical successes can be defended by the usual reference to the essential unfathomableness of religious mysteries and the repudiation of idle curiosity in favour of the eternal wisdom of the Church and its abiding tradition. 'It is not right to dissolve the ancient traditions of the Faith, which have come down to us from the holy apostles themselves; it is wrong to break them up with our exaggerated cleverness and wrong to try to overcome what transcends reason with inquiries carried to extremes or even frivolously to declare with certain artists in definition: this is right; this is wrong. What is needed and blessed is rather to leave the all-knowing God to make his own decisions and not criticize with wanton audacity what he has deemed good' (*De Fide Recta ad Imper.* 17, *ACO* I, 1, p. 53, 10).

Here we see the limitations, or, if you like, the individuality of Cyril as a teacher of the Church. As we have seen, Cyril in fact wanted to be a theologian. But for him theology no longer is answerable only to itself within the Church. It has become the sphere of the teaching office and must in all circumstances comply with the traditions of the Church. No one before Cyril had emphasized the importance of the 'Fathers' so indefatigably. He was convinced that they had 'not left out or overlooked anything vital' at all and that everyone who accepted the orthodox Faith would find in their 'confessions and interpretations' useful material with which to refute 'all heresy and godless insolence' (*De Symb.* 4, *ACO* I, 4, 4, p. 50, 22). He initiated the practice of deciding questions of belief not solely on the basis of the Bible but with the aid of appropriate quotations and collections of quotations from acknowledged authorities and above all from the great Athanasius. This was the

12

purpose of his own writing, which was based from the beginning so largely on quotations and excerpts. This was now regarded as the truly 'royal way' of theology: 'to defer on every issue to the confessions of the holy Fathers, which came about through the inspiration of the Holy Spirit; and to keep firmly in mind the train of their thoughts' (*Ep. 17*, 3, *ACO* I, 1, 1, p. 35, 12). This meant that the creative age of the theology of the early Church had come to an end. In virtue of this theological programme, Cyril can be called the first of the Byzantine scholastics. In the Greek world he was the last of the Fathers of the Church because, strictly speaking, he no longer had any desire to be one. For that reason, he was regarded, as later theologians said, as the 'guardian of accuracy' (Eulog. Al. in Photios, *Bibl. Cod.* 230) and forms the final 'seal of the Fathers' (Anastas. Sin., *viae dux 7*).

THE END OF THE AGE OF THE GREEK FATHERS

WHEN we review the series of pre- and post-Nicene Fathers we are surprised by the rich variety of quite different characters, independent points of view, individual ways of life, and forms of expression. It was a great field of intellectual life with which they were concerned for three centuries, which they tackled, conquered, penetrated, and moulded theologically. Their work was not done according to a fixed plan but in the awareness of a very definite common cause and with a sense of responsibility to a freedom of belief in which reason was respected. All the Fathers we have studied thought of themselves as members of the one 'Catholic' Church and strove to serve the preaching of the gospel, the truth of God, and of the Faith.

The Bible and the revelation of Christ to which the Bible bears witness formed the natural foundation, the common point of departure, and the norm of all their work and research. Starting from these foundations, they sought to ward off 'errors' and prevent a dissolution and disintegration of the Church from within. At the same time, however, they looked outwards into the world and considered its moral and philosophical problems. Everything had to be won for the Logos of God, purified by him and understood anew in him. Their theology was also intended to be a 'philosophy'; it was anti-heretical and missionary, polemical and apologetic in intention at one and the same time. There is sometimes a touch of naïveté about its fresh confidence in victory, but in loyalty to 'the one thing needful' it remains lively and flexible, advances and, in spite of internal and external difficulties, maintains its superiority over its enemies, and finally emerges victorious.

The age of the Fathers of the Church came to an end for various reasons: general, political, sociological, cultural and biological. As with every ultimate historical question, there can be no completely conclusive explanation. We have already touched on the matter in the Introduction and in the course of our description have given our attention first and foremost to the presuppositions underlying the teaching of the Church. A slow process of change took place in the conception of theology and the position of teachers in the Church, which was the inevitable result of their own work and influence. These changes in any case acquire from our point of view an essential and decisive significance. From the very beginning belief in the Bible as the document of divine revelation and high regard for 'natural' reason had gone hand in hand with a frank acceptance of ecclesiastical authority and tradition. The strengthening of these ties and of their political importance, and the progressive systematization of the theological inheritance, which was becoming ever richer and increasingly complex, contributed very largely to the gradual stagnation of intellectual life and the consequent end of the 'classical' patristic age.

We can do no more here than merely outline this process. The turning-point which was reached with the accession of Constantine and the rise of the Imperial Church, closely bound up with the State and public order, undoubtedly constitutes the most significant moment in the process of development. It brought new political and legal ties which strengthened earlier tendencies, and at the same time brought some dangerous developments which involved a stricter regard for dogmatic unity and ecclesiastical decisions. For the first time, in the East the 'Creed' was put forward as a dogmatic and legal standard binding on the Church as a whole. The victory of Nicene orthodoxy was won 'in this sign'. Both Athanasius and Basil persistently appealed to the decision of Nicaea, but they had no wish to go beyond the Nicene Creed and they assiduously avoided adding any further dogmatic formulations. In Ephesus too (431) the old Creed, which had simply been 'extended' in Constantinople in 381, was retained, and even in Chalcedon (451) a tough battle was fought, which failed in the end, to prevent a new formulation of the Faith. On the other hand, however, efforts had been under way for a long time to define more clearly and make more intelligible the fluid conception of the 'genuine' and authoritative tradition. The Emperor Theodosius the Great took the first step in this direction when he appointed to prepare the reorganization of the Eastern Churches a group of theologians, by whom the rest were to be guided (380–81). Soon afterwards, in 383, reference was made to earlier, no longer living, Fathers who had proclaimed the truth in the 'right' way and were recognized by the Church. Later, however, this summary reference to the Fathers was not deemed sufficient. Particular, authoritative writings of Athanasius and other teachers and Fathers were singled out to serve as criteria. These too were supplanted in the following period by the anthologies, which were easier to handle: collections of quotations on dogmatics the selection of which varied according to the passing needs of theological controversy and which brought together genuine quotations torn from their original contexts with a great deal of adulterated and unauthentic material. It was above all Cyril of Alexandria who used this method in his controversies and made it predominant. For analogous practical reasons the method was also introduced in jurisprudence about the same time. The imperial 'Quotation Law' of 426 bound the administration of justice quite formally to particular acknowledged authorities of the past. The final condemnation of Origen by Justinian in 543 brought the effort of Church and State to achieve a standardization of tradition to a conclusion.

As the process of standardization advanced, so the keenness and capacity for independent theological research and teaching waned. Anyone who wanted to say something really new was most likely to say it under a false flag. Thus, in the latter part of the fourth century, the Apollinarians had covered up their

12 *a*

condemned literature with the name of St. Athanasius. About the turn of the fifth to the sixth century a Monophysite put into circulation his mystical Neoplatonic ideas about the Church and the liturgy under the cloak of Dionysius the Areopagite (Acts xvii. 34). At a religious discussion which took place in Constantinople in 532 his writings were still rejected as unauthentic, but in the following age they became established. It was inevitable that thanks to this sanctifying of the ecclesiastic tradition the Bible itself was pushed more and more into the background. Official theology no longer responded to its revolutionizing force. It is true that it was revived in the opening phases of monasticism, and for that very reason the monks distrusted all dogmatics and official theology. The most important critic of previous developments, the leader of the Euchite (Messalian) movement, Simeon of Mesopotamia, who died at the close of the fourth century, was condemned as a heretic, and he survives only under a false name as (Pseudo-)'Macarius'.

Another factor was the confusion and complications inherent in the dogmatic tradition itself. The fiction of an unbroken uniformity is in contradiction to the truth and had to be preserved by an ever-increasing expenditure of formalistic ingenuity. The effect of the Council of Chalcedon was particularly catastrophic in this respect. It meant a serious defeat for the Alexandrian theology which had triumphed twenty years previously in Ephesus. But this fact was concealed, since Cyril, the victor of Ephesus, was lauded in Chalcedon with great enthusiasm and set alongside the totally different Bishop Leo of Rome. And so there arose, soon afterwards, the controversy about the interpretation of the Chalcedonian Definition which was concluded a hundred years later under Justinian in a way (Alexandrian Monophysite) that makes nonsense historically and was then converted into a dogma by a new ecumenical Council in Constantinople in 553.

Similar difficulties and artificial harmonizations affected the propositions and methods of philosophy, as if these were the equally traditional presuppositions for theology and dogma.

The earlier Fathers of the Church had all been, more or less, pure Platonists, and the doctrine of the Trinity had been originally conceived in Platonic-Neoplatonic terms. In the fifth and sixth centuries Aristotelian logic began to make its mark and was combined with the Neoplatonic traditions, inside and outside theology. Thus there came into being a terrifyingly complicated apparatus which, however, did not function according to its own laws but was twisted to suit the particular metaphysical and theological principles which it was intended to justify.

The result of all these changes was Byzantine scholasticism, a scientific theology so heavily armoured that only the most learned specialists, monks, and clerics could find their way about. It took a man like Maximus the Confessor (d. 662), and his vigour of mind and faith, to fight in this armour and still make himself understood, setting the whole Church in motion and revealing the sublime errors of Monotheletism as errors of faith. Normally, dogmatics failed to make any impact on everyday piety. The problems of mysticism and of the controversy about images were artfully, but only at a later stage, linked up with doctrine and so brought to a decision. In this connection, the most important name is John of Damascus, who died in 749, since in him the whole historical development of dogmatic thought came to an end in the East. Under the protection of Islamic power he conducted a controversy against the iconoclastic Emperors of Byzantium and composed in a typical combination of cleverness and stupidity the huge dogmatic collection called *The Fount of Wisdom*, which became the model for innumerable later manuals, even in the West. It includes, before getting down to theology proper, an introduction on the history of philosophical concepts, a 'Dialectic', and a heresiology compiled from innumerable earlier authors. Every feasible question is put in its 'rightful' and due place.

Greek theology was gradually suffocated by its own traditionalism. No more or less justified admiration for its conceptual refinements, profundity, and sublimity can alter that fact. The

Fathers had become so holy that in the end they could no longer beget any sons who were their equals in vitality. Theology lived its own life in constant reference to the past and lost all direct contact with the Bible and with life outside or different from itself. In 529 Justinian closed the school in Athens, and the last pagan philosophers left the Empire. Christian missionaries penetrated only into areas where they were desired on political grounds and where the cultural superiority of the Empire smoothed the way for them. The Church was powerless against Islam, and the enormous losses which it suffered at its hands were by no means entirely due to external military causes. It is most striking that the new theological life that came into being in the West in the fourth and fifth centuries had no influence in the East, whereas the West was always open to the influence of Greek theology. Perhaps it was just this feeling of distance from its origins, the need to listen and grow in awareness of the genuine historical differences, which gave Latin theology its power of independent life, although to begin with it owed everything to the Greeks. But the latter had long since thought of themselves as having attained their final goal. Imprisoned in their own territorial and cultural confines, their Church rested upon its own perfection. It trusted in an unchanging and indestructible continuity with the apostles and Fathers of the past whose achievements it admired so much that it failed to observe the changing nature of the problems which faced theology. It preserved their intellectual inheritance without doing anything to renew it.

CHRONOLOGICAL TABLE

138–61	Emperor Antoninus Pius	144	Marcion breaks with Rome
161–80	Emperor Marcus Aurelius	circa 165	Death of Justin
		177–78	Irenaeus Bishop of Lyons
202	Septimius Severus forbids conversion to Christianity	202–03	Clement leaves Alexandria; Origen head of the catechetical school in Alexandria
		230–31	Origen moves to Caesarea in Palestine
		235	Death of Hippolytus of Rome
250–51	Persecution of Christians by Decius		
255–59	Persecution of Christians by Valerian	253–54	Death of Origen
		circa 270	Death of Gregory Thaumaturgus
303	Beginning of the great persecution of the Christians under Diocletian		
		309?	Death of Pamphilus
324	Constantine the Great sole ruler		
325	Council of Nicaea		
		328	Athanasius Bishop of Alexandria
337	Death of Constantine the Great		
		339	Death of Eusebius of Caesarea
		356	Antony's death at age of 105

361–63   Emperor Julian

                                        373   Death of Athanasius

379–95   Emperor Theodosius   379   Death of Basil the
          the Great   Great

     381   Council of Constanti-
            nople   389–90   Death of Gregory of
                                      Nazianzus

                           394   Death of Gregory of
                                      Nyssa

395–408   Emperor Arcadius   398   Chrysostom Bishop of
                                      Constantinople

     403   Synod of the Oak   407   Death of Chrysostom
408–50   Emperor Theodosius II

                           410   Synesius Bishop of
                                      Ptolemaïs

                           412   Cyril Bishop of Alex-
                                    andria

                           415   Murder of Hypatia

     431   Council of Ephesus

                           444   Death of Cyril of Alex-
     451   Council of Chalcedon   andria

BIBLIOGRAPHY

INTRODUCTION

The surviving works of the earlier Greek Fathers of the Church are to be found almost complete in the critical editions of *Die griechischen christlichen Schriftsteller der ersten drei Jahrhunderte*, published by the Berlin Academy from 1897 onwards. For the later Fathers the very often inferior reprints by J. P. Migne are still indispensable: *Patrologiae cursus completus, Series Graeca* (with Latin translations), Paris, 1857 ff. A large selection of English translations is provided in Roberts and Donaldson, *The Ante-Nicene Christian Library* (Edinburgh, 1867–71); Schaff and Wace, *A Select Library of Nicene and Post-Nicene Fathers of the Christian Church* (Oxford and New York, 1886–1900); Quasten and Plumpe (later Quasten and Burghardt), *Ancient Christian Writers* (Westminster, Md. and London, 1946 ff.); Schopp, *The Fathers of the Church* (New York, 1947 ff.); Baillie, McNeill, Van Dusen, *The Library of Christian Classics* (London and Philadelphia, 1953 ff.).

The following is a selection of the most important patristic handbooks which will help the interested reader to explore the subject further. A. v. Harnack's *Geschichte der altchristlichen Literatur bis Eusebius* did not get beyond the preliminary parts I (*Überlieferung und Bestand*, 1893) and II (*Chronologie*, 1897–1904). O. Bardenhewer's assiduous *Geschichte der altkirchlichen Literatur*, I–V (1913–1932), is the most complete of the earlier compilations. There is a concise but excellent *Patrology* by Altaner (E. T., Edinburgh, 1958). Also in English there is, above all, the *Patrology* in several volumes by J. Quasten (Utrecht, 1950 ff.) and there are E. J. Goodspeed, *A History of Early Christian Literature* (Chicago, 1942) and, for the Greeks, J. M. Campbell, *The Greek Fathers* (London and New York, 1929).

The most important complete accounts of the dogmatic history of Greek antiquity are: A. v. Harnack, *History of Dogma*, I–VII (1894–99); R. Seeberg, *Lehrbuch der Dogmengeschichte* (Leipzig, 1920 ff.); Fr. Loofs, *Leitfaden zum Studium der Dogmengeschichte*,

I–II, 5th ed., edited by K. Aland (1950–53); J. Tixeront, *Histoire des dogmes* (1930[11], English translation, St. Louis and London, 1930 ff.).

Reference should be made to the following general histories of the Church: L. Duchesne, *Early History of the Christian Church* (London, 1909–24); K. Müller, *Kirchengeschichte*, I, 1 (3rd ed., 1941, in collaboration with H. v. Campenhausen); B. J. Kidd, *A History of the Church to A.D. 461* (Oxford, 1922); J. Lebreton and J. Zeiller, *The History of the Primitive Church* (tr. from the French) (New York, 1949); H. Lietzmann, *Geschichte der alten Kirche*, English translation by B. L. Wolff (New York, 1937 ff.); and the first four volumes of the Catholic compilation, *Histoire de l'Église*, edited by Fliche and Martin (Paris, 1935 ff.).

Ch. I—JUSTIN

W. Schmid is preparing a new edition of Justin's *Apology*. The many existing editions of his writings are inadequate. Research on Justin has usually been associated with more far-reaching studies of the apologists in general or limited to articles. Reference may be made to J. Geffcken, *Zwei griechische Apologeten* (1907), and A. von Ungern-Sternberg, *Der traditionelle Schriftbeweis 'de Christo' und 'de evangelio' in der alten Kirche* (1913). Comprehensive accounts of Justin's theology have been given by M. v. Engelhardt, *Das Christentum Justins des Märtyrers* (1878), and E. R. Goodenough, *The Theology of Justin Martyr* (Jena, 1923). W. Schmid, 'Die Textüberlieferung der Apologie des Justin', *Zeitschr. f. neutest. Wissensch.*, 40 (1941), 87 ff., and 'Frühe Apologetik und Platonismus', *Festschrift Otto Regenbogen* (1952), 163 ff., are important for the light they throw on Justin's historical position.

Ch. II—IRENAEUS

The editions of the *Refutation and Overthrow of Gnosis, Falsely So Called* (quoted as *adversus haereses*) by A. Stieren (1848–53) and W. W. Harvey (Cambridge, 1857), which were excellent in their time, are still usable. F. Sagnard has undertaken a new edition with a French translation (Paris, 1952). *The Demonstration of the Apostolic Preaching* was published by K. Ter-Mekerttschian and E. Ter-Minassiantz in 1907 in Armenian with a German translation. It has also appeared in English and French translations in the *Patrologia Orientalis*, 12, 5 (Paris, 1919).

Of fundamental importance for the source problem is the (not uncontested) analysis in Fr. Loofs, *Theophilus von Antiochien und die anderen theologischen Quellen bei Irenäus* (1930). For his theological and ecclesiastical thought cf. F. R. M. Hitchcock, *Irenaeus of Lugdunum, A Study of His Teaching* (Cambridge, 1914), J. Lawson, *The Biblical Theology of St. Irenaeus* (London, 1948), and H. v. Campenhausen, *Kirchliches Amt und geistliche Vollmacht in den ersten drei Jahrhunderten* (1953), pp. 185 ff.

Ch. III—CLEMENT OF ALEXANDRIA

The works of Clement were published by O. Stählin in an excellent edition in the *Griechische christliche Kirchenväter*, 1905–09; see also the Index published in 1936 and the German translation in the *Bibliothek der Kirchenväter* (1934–38) with an Introduction and a new revision of the text. Various volumes of the collection *Sources chrétiennes* (Paris, 1949 ff.) provide a revised text with a French translation. See also the English translation by W. Wilson in the *Ante-Nicene Fathers* (1887). There are English editions of *Stromateis* VII by Hort and Mayor (London, 1903) and *Protrepticus* and *Quis Dives Salvetur* by Butterworth (London and Cambridge, Mass., 1919).

The literature on Clement is immense and ever-growing. The most important contributions are as follows: Bigg, *The Christian Platonists of Alexandria* (ed. Brightman, London, 1913); W. Bousset, *Jüdisch-christlicher Schulbetrieb in Alexandria und Rom. Literarische Untersuchungen zu Philo und Clemens von Alexandria* (1915); J. Munck, *Untersuchungen über Clemens von Alexandria* (1933); G. Lazzati, *Introduzione allo studio di Clemente Alessandrino* (Milan, 1939).

On the problems of his theology and intellectual outlook see: F. R. M. Hitchcock, *Clement of Alexandria* (London, 1899); E. Molland, *The Conception of the Gospel in Alexandrian Theology* (Oslo, 1938); W. Völker, *Der wahre Gnostiker nach Clemens Alexandrinus* (1952); H. v. Campenhausen, *Kirchliches Amt und geistliche Vollmacht in den ersten drei Jahrhunderten* (1953), pp. 215 ff.

Ch. IV—ORIGEN

The old editions of de la Rue (1733–59) and Lommatzsch (1831–48) are no longer adequate and have been progressively replaced since 1899 by the editions of the Berlin Academy in the *Griechische christliche Schriftsteller*. The newly-discovered record of a conversation,

Entretien d'Origène avec Héraclide, edited by Jean Scherer (Paris, 1949) is important.

The literature on Origen is enormous; but there has been no satisfactory complete account of him since the earlier exposition of E. R. Redepenning (1841–46), which contains much material, and the somewhat too elegant, more recent study by E. de Faye (3 vols., Paris, 1923–28).

For the early period see: R. Cadiou (translated by J. A. Southwell), *Origen. His Life at Alexandria* (St. Louis and London, 1944).

Of fundamental importance for his relationship to contemporary philosophy: Hal Koch, *Pronoia und Paideusis, Studien über Origenes und sein Verhältnis zum Platonismus* (1932). A. Miura-Stange, *Celsus und Origenes, das Gemeinsame ihrer Weltanschauung* (1926), is also useful. W. Völker, *Das Vollkommenheitsideal des Origenes* (1931), attempts to interpret Origen from the standpoint of his piety and alleged mysticism. Cf. H. Jonas, 'Die origenistische Spekulation und die Mystik', *Theol. Zeitschr.*, 5 (1949), 24 ff.

French research on Origen has been particularly fruitful: R. Cadiou, *La Jeunesse d'Origène* (Paris, 1935); J. Daniélou, *Origène* (Paris, 1950); H. de Lubac, *Histoire et esprit. L'Intelligence de l'écriture d'après Origène* (Paris, 1950); Fr. Bertrand, *Mystique de Jésus chez Origène* (Paris, 1951); H. Crouzel, *Théologie de l'image de Dieu chez Origène* (Paris, 1956).

The danger lies in too much stress being laid on the specifically ecclesiastical and sacramental 'Catholic' aspects. The best objective introduction is provided by Hal Koch, art. 'Origen' in Pauly-Wissowa-Kroll's *Realencyklopädie*, XVIII, 1 (1939), 1036 ff.

Ch. V—EUSEBIUS OF CAESAREA

The critical edition in the *Griechische christliche Schriftsteller* has not yet been concluded. Above all, the edition of the *Church History* (1903–09) by Ed. Schwartz (with Rufinus's Latin translation edited by Th. Mommsen), of which a 'short edition' has also appeared (3rd edition, 1922; reprinted, 1952), is of fundamental importance. Schwartz was also responsible for the masterly comprehensive article on Eusebius in Pauly-Wissowa-Kroll's *Realencycklopädie*, VI, 1 (1907), 1370 ff. There are English translations by A. C. McGiffert (London, 1890), Lake (London, 1927–28) and an important article by Headlam in the *J.T.S.* IV (1903), 93, 'The editions and MSS of Eusebius'.

H. Berkhof's *Die Theologie des Eusebius von Caesarea* (1939) provides an excellent exposition. On the political and theological background cf. also H. Eger, 'Kaiser und Kirche in der Geschichtstheologie Eusebs von Caesarea', *Zeitschr. f. neutest. Wissensch.*, 38 (1939), 97 ff.; Joh. Straub, *Vom Herrscherideal der Spätantike* (1939), and the brilliant but theologically questionable study by E. Peterson, *Der Monotheismus als politisches Problem. Ein Beitrag zur Geschichte der politischen Theologie im Imperium Romanum* (1935). The best English works are Lawlor, *Eusebiana* (Oxford, 1912) and Stevenson, *Studies in Eusebius* (Cambridge, 1929).

CH. VI—ATHANASIUS

H.-G. Opitz made a start on a new edition of the works of Athanasius in 1934; it is to be continued by W. Schneemelcher. An important guide to the study of Athanasius is provided by Guido Müller's *Lexicon Athanasianum* (1952), which also serves as a concordance.

There is as yet no exhaustive biography of Athanasius. F. L. Cross, *The Study of Athanasius* (Oxford, 1945), provides a good introduction.

The essays by Ed. Schwartz, 'Zur Geschichte des Athanasios', in the *Göttinger gelehrte Anzeigen* (1904–11; cf. also *Kaiser Konstantin und die christliche Kirche*, 1936²) are still important.

A survey of the complicated ecclesiastical political struggles is provided by H. Lietzmann's fascinating exposition in the third volume of his *Geschichte der alten Kirche* (1953²) (English translation, 1937–1951).

The development of Athanasius's views on ecclesiastical law is studied in the Giessen dissertation by K. F. Hagel, *Kirche und Kaisertum in Lehre und Leben des Athanasius* (1933), and K. M. Setton, *Christian Attitude Towards the Emperor in the Fourth Century* (New York, 1941).

For the much discussed *Vita Antonii* it is enough to refer to the most recent study by H. Dörries, 'Die Vita Antonii als Geschichtsquelle' (in the *Göttinger gelehrte Anzeigen*, 1949).

CH. VII—BASIL THE GREAT

There is no complete critical edition of the writings of Basil, nor is there a worthy biography.

A sound and convenient survey of the present state of research is provided by the Basel theological dissertation by L. Vischer, *Basilius der Grosse, Untersuchungen zu einem Kirchenvater des 4. Jahrhunderts* (1953). There are also a great number of more or less valuable studies of particular aspects of his theology and work, especially his attitude to classical culture. On Basil's ascetic theory, cf. D. Amand, *L'Ascèse monastique de S. Basile* (1949) and Clarke, *St. Basil the Great*, A Study in Monasticism (Cambridge, 1913); on his view of the State, G. F. Reilly, *Imperium and Sacerdotium According to St. Basil the Great* (theol. diss., Washington, 1945); on the Antiochene schism, F. Cavallera, *Le Schisme d'Antioche* (Paris, 1905); and for his stand on dogma, K. Holl, *Amphilochius von Ikonium in seinem Verhältnis zu den grossen Kappadoziern* (1904), and more recently, B. Schewe, *Basilius der Grosse als Theologe* (diss., Nymwegen, 1943) and, particularly important, Dörries, *De spiritu sancto, der Beitrag des Basilius zum Abschluss des trinitarischen Dogmas* (1956). More general is Fox, *The Life and Times of St. Basil the Great as revealed in his Works* (Washington, 1939). The correct Greek spelling of the name is Basileios; it was pronounced by then Vasilios.

Ch. VIII—GREGORY OF NAZIANZUS

In the case of Gregory of Nazianzus we are still dependent on the reprint of his works in Migne's *Patrologia graeco-latina*. The old, no longer adequate biography by C. Ullmann, *Gregorius von Nazianz, der Theologe* (1867²), has been joined by more recent expositions, especially in French, which concentrate on one or another aspect of his character: M. Guignet, *S. Grégoire de Nazianze orateur et épistolier* (Paris, 1911); P. Gallay, *La Vie de S. Grégoire* (Paris, 1943), and the very systematic study by J. Plaignieux, *S. Grégoire de Nazianze, théologien* (Paris, 1952).

Of the innumerable studies of Gregory's attitude to ancient literature and culture, special mention should be made of H. M. Werhahn's richly annotated edition of Gregory's Σύγκρισις βίων (1953). B. Wyss, 'Gregor von Nazianz. Ein griechisch-christlicher Dichter des 4. Jahrhunderts' (*Mus. Helvet.*, 6, 1949), provides the liveliest description of Gregory's personality, as well as useful information on points of detail. The best theological assessment is still to be found, in my opinion, in K. Holl, *Amphilochius von Ikonium in seinem Verhältnis zu den grossen Kappadoziern* (1904), except that even Holl does not perhaps always pay enough attention to the intensely

rhetorical character of Gregory's dogmatic formulations and therefore takes some things all too literally and seriously.

Ch. IX—GREGORY OF NYSSA

Werner Jaeger's critical edition of the works of Gregory (the letters
edited by G. Pasquali) began in 1921, replacing the quite inadequate
texts that appear in Migne. To some extent, however, I have quoted
from Migne, since his columns are also referred to in the margin of
Jaeger's edition.

There have been many studies of Gregory's mysticism and religious thought in recent times. In most cases special stress has been
laid on the 'Christian' content of his thought, as compared with the
obviously Neoplatonic elements. Special mention should be made
of: H. F. Cherniss, *The Platonism of Gregory of Nyssa* (Berkeley,
1930); H. U. von Balthasar, *Présence et Pensée. Essai sur la philosophie
religieuse de Grégoire de Nysse* (Paris, 1942); A. Lieske, 'Die Theologie der Christusmystik Gregors von Nyssa', in *Zeitschr. f. kath.
Theologie*, 70 (1948), 49 ff.; 129 ff.; 315 ff., and, in particular, the
comprehensive work by J. Daniélou, *Platonisme et théologie mystique.
Essai sur la doctrine spirituelle de Saint Grégoire de Nysse* (Paris, 1954²);
and also his article, 'La Résurrection des corps chez Grégoire de
Nysse', *Vigil. Christ.*, 7 (1953), 154 ff. A recent work is W. Völker,
Gregor von Nyssa als Mystiker (1955).

The brilliant study by J. Gaïth, *La Conception de la liberté chez Grégoire de Nysse* (Paris, 1953), suffers somewhat from the one-sidedly
philosophical and systematic approach. A limited theme but one
that is central in Gregory's thought is dealt with by R. Leys,
L'Image de Dieu chez Saint Grégoire de Nysse. Esquisse d'une doctrine
(Brussels, Paris, 1951), and H. Merki, ʽΟΜΟΙΩΣΙΣ ΘΕΩΙ. *Von der
platonischen Angleichung an Gott zur Gottähnlichkeit bei Gregor von
Nyssa* (Freiburg, Switzerland, 1952), which is a particularly fruitful
study from the philological and historical points of view.

Ch. X—SYNESIUS OF CYRENE

The earlier editions of Synesius have been superseded, for the letters
by R. Hercher, *Epistolographi Graeci* (Paris, 1873), 638–739; for the
hymns and other writings by the Roman edition begun in 1939 by
N. Terzaghi, *Synesii Cyrenensis hymni et opuscula*. English translation
by A. Fitzgerald of *Letters* (London, 1926), *Essays and Hymns* (2 vols.,
London, 1930).

G. Grützmacher provided a solid biography in his *Synesios von Kyrene—ein Charakterbild aus dem Untergang des Hellenentums* (1913) and, more recently, Chr. Lacombrade, *Synesios de Cyrène, Hellène et chrétien* (Paris, 1951), in which all the earlier literature is listed. English studies of his life and works by Alice Gardner, in *The Fathers for English Readers* series (London, 1886); J. C. Nicol, *Synesius of Cyrene. His Life and Writings* (Cambridge, 1887); and W. S. Crawford, *Synesius the Hellene* (London, 1901).

J. C. Pando, 'The Life and Times of Synesius of Cyrene' (Catholic University of America, *Patristic Studies*, Vol. 63, Washington, 1940), is more of a compilation.

Ch. XI—JOHN CHRYSOSTOM

No complete edition has been attempted since the edition by Montfaucon (1718–38), which was reprinted, with additions, by Migne. The editions of particular works are also sparse and unimportant. For much of the text the best edition is still that of Savile (8 vols. Eton, 1612).

A prolix biography in two volumes in which all the literature is listed was provided by Chr. Baur in *Der heilige Johannes Chrysostomus und seine Zeit* (1929–30). Especially important for chronology is de Tillemont, *Mémoires pour servir à l'histoire ecclésiastique des six premiers siècles*, Vol. IX (Paris, 1706). Mention should also be made of V. Schultze's exposition in the third volume of his *Early Christian Cities and Landscapes* (1930), which deals with Antioch. An important source for the biography of Chrysostom is Palladius's *Dialogus de Vita S. Joannis Chrysostomi*, which appeared in an excellent edition by P. R. Coleman-Norton in Cambridge in 1928. English lives by Stephens, *St John Chrysostom, his Life and Times* (London, 1880[2]) and (more popular) Bush, *The Life and Times of Chrysostom* (London, 1885).

There are not many theological studies of his work; one of the best is G. Fittkau's 'Der Begriff des Mysteriums bei Johannes Chrysostomos' (*Theophaneia*, IX, Bonn, 1953).

Ch. XII—CYRIL OF ALEXANDRIA

The only complete edition of Cyril's works, by Joh. Aubertus (1638), was reprinted by Migne in *Patr. graeca*, 68–77.

His anti-Nestorian writings may now be found almost complete in the first volume of the *Acta conciliorum oecumenicorum* (*ACO*), by Ed. Schwartz.

The latter's introductions and scattered treatises have made the best contribution to explaining the political proceedings in the Church. See especially *Cyrill und der Mönch Viktor* (1928).

There is no adequate modern biography of Cyril.

The following is important for the light it throws on his theological position within the Alexandrian tradition: J. Liébaert, *La Doctrine christologique de Saint Cyrille d'Alexandrie avant la querelle nestorienne* (Lille, 1951). A. Kerrigan, *St. Cyril of Alexandria, Interpreter of the Old Testament* (Rome, 1952), deals with his methods of exegesis. There is much material too in H. du Manoir de Juaye, *Dogme et spiritualité chez Saint Cyrille d'Alexandrie* (Paris, 1944).

INDEX OF PROPER NAMES

Alexander, Bp. of Alexandria, 70, 71
Alexander, Cappadocian Bp., 36
Ambrosius, 50
Ammonius Saccas, 40
Amphilochius, Bp. of Iconium, 103
Andronicus, 137
Anthony, 82
Antoninus Pius, 13
Apollinaris, Bp. of Laodicea, 161
Apollophanes, 40
Arcadius, 130, 148, 150, 152, 154, 157
Aristides, 6
Arius, 66, 67, 70, 71, 73, 161
Athanasius, 69-83, 84, 85, 93, 96, 97, 116, 158, 159, 160, 163, 168, 169, 172, 173, 174
Athenagoras, 6
Augustine, 82

Basil the Great, 84-100, 101, 102, 103, 104, 105, 107, 108, 109, 113, 114, 115, 116, 117, 118, 119, 121, 122, 125, 128, 133, 138, 143, 168, 172

Caesarius, 109
Celestine I, Bp. of Rome, 165
Celsus, 55
Chrysostom, John, 140-57, 158, 159, 160, 162, 163
Clement of Alexandria, 2, 25-36, 39, 42, 48, 49, 51, 52, 81, 88, 99, 120
Constantine, 63, 64, 65, 67, 71, 73, 74, 75, 172
Constantius, 75, 77, 79, 105
Crescens, 10, 14
Cronius, 40
Cyril, Bp. of Alexandria, 2, 158-70, 173, 174

Damasus I, Bp. of Rome, 96
Decius, 55
Demetrius, Bp. of Alexandria, 39, 40, 50, 51, 52, 53, 54, 69, 158
Didymus, 160
Dio Chrysostom of Prusa, 127
Diodorus, Bp. of Tarsus, 143
Dionysius, Bp. of Alexandria, 69
Dionysius the Areopagite, 174

Epiphanius, Bp. of Salamis, 152
Eudoxia, 150, 151, 152, 153, 154
Eunomius, 122, 161
Eusebius, Bp. of Caesarea in Cappadocia, 90
Eusebius, Bp. of Caesarea in Palestine, 16, 38, 57-68, 69, 84, 99
Eustathius, Bp. of Sebaste, 87, 88, 90
Eutropius, 148, 151

Gregory of Nazianzus, 86, 89, 101-114, 115, 116, 117, 118, 122, 125, 127, 128, 142, 147
Gregory, Bp. of Nyssa, 97, 101, 114, 115-25, 138
Gregory Thaumaturgus, 49-50, 85

Heraclitus, 9
Heraklas, Bp. of Alexandria, 40
Hippolytus of Rome, 37, 38
Homer, 86, 103
Hypatia, 128, 129, 130, 138, 161

Irenaeus, 16-24, 37, 38, 72, 99

John, Bp. of Antioch, 167
John Chrysostom (see Chrysostom, John)
John of Damascus, 175
Julia Mammaea, 50
Julian the Apostate, 79, 80, 105, 161

Justin, 5-15, 16, 19, 23, 25, 26, 39, 48, 59, 99
Justinian, 173, 174, 176

Leo I, Bp. of Rome, 174
Leonides, 39
Libanius, 86, 117
Longinus, 40

(Pseudo-)'Macarius', 174
Macrina, 86, 118, 119
Marcion, 19
Maximinus, 86
Maximus, 110, 111
Maximus the Confessor, 175
Meletius, Bp. of Antioch, 96, 97, 111, 144
Melitius, Bp. of Lycopolis, 70
Moderatus, 40
Musonius, Bp. of Neo-Caesarea, 100

Nectarius, Bp. of Constantinople, 147
Nestorius, 162, 163, 164, 165, 166, 167, 168
Nicomachus, 40
Numenius, 40

Origen, 2, 37-56, 57, 58, 60, 66, 69, 72, 75, 81, 85, 88, 89, 99, 117, 121, 122, 123, 124, 160, 173

Pamphilus, 57, 58
Pantaenus, 26, 36

Paulinus, 111
Pelagius, 144
Philip the Arab, 50
Philo, 42, 117, 123
Pierius, 57
Plato, 8, 11, 27, 33, 86, 117, 118, 131
Plotinus, 38, 40, 43, 117, 121
Polycarp, 17
Porphyry, 40, 129
Pulcheria, 165

Quadratus, 6

Rusticus, 14

Septimus Severus, 36
Simeon of Mesopotamia, 174
Socrates, 9
Synesius, 126-39

Tatian, 6
Tertullian, 15
Theodosius I, the Great, 80, 97, 109, 110, 119, 147, 173
Theodosius II, 157, 165
Theophilus, Bp. of Alexandria, 134, 136, 148, 151, 152, 154, 158, 159
Theosebia, 117
Timotheus, 159

Valens, 92, 109, 143
Vespasian, 6
Victor I, Bp. of Rome, 18